Nothing Is Hidden

Nothing Is Hidden

Essays on Zen Master Dōgen's Instructions for the Cook

Edited by
Jisho Warner, Shōhaku Okumura,
John McRae, and Taigen Dan Leighton

WEATHERHILL
New York · Tokyo

鋤頭作自道心体他不是空還待誰
辨食法門何處會打米一片汗流時

敬題典座教訓參究公案偈頌會松峯○□慧忍玉衲

In Praise of *Instructions for the Cook*

Egyoku Hata, abbot of Eiheiji (1976–85)

The pot is my head,
Rolled up the sleeves, the mind of the Way.
Others are not me,
For whom should I wait?

Where will I meet
The dharma of cooking?
All becomes one
As the sweat pours down.

鍋頭作自道心襷　鍋頭を自と作し、道心を襷とす
他不是吾還待誰　他は是れ吾ならず、また誰をか待たん
辦食法門何処會　辦食の法門、いずれの処にか會す
打成一片汗流時　打成一片、汗流るる時

First edition, 2001

Published by Weatherhill, Inc.
41 Monroe Turnpike
Trumbull, CT 06611

Protected by copyright under the terms of the International Copyright Union; all rights reserved. Except for fair use in book reviews, no part of this book may be reproduced for any reason by any means, including any method of photographic reproduction, without permission of the publisher. Printed in the United States.

Library of Congress Cataloging-in-Publication Data available upon request.

Contents

Foreword
Dōgen in the Twenty-first Century · *Ekiho Miyazaki*   9

Introduction
Sharing Dōgen's World   12

Part I: Dōgen's Instructions for the Cook

Instructions for the Cook · translated by *Griffith Foulk*   21

An Introductory Guide to *Instructions for the Cook* · *Renpō Niwa*   41

Part II: Practice for Your Whole Life

A Monk's Mouth Is Like an Oven · *Shundō Aoyama*   49

Spreading the Dharma, Engaging Your Life · *Dainin Katagiri*   59

Mendicant Practice in Buddha's World · *Zengan Hashimoto*   66

Kitchen Kōans · *Kōryō Shinno*   75

Magnanimous Mind · *Kōdō Kurebayashi*   83

Just Cooking, Just Sitting · *Kōshō Uchiyama*   93

Part III: Roots of Mealtime Practice

Eating Customs in the Early Sangha in India · *Kōgen Mizuno*   105

Rules for Meals in China · *Hisao Shinohara*   116

Appendices

Glossary   127

Chinese and Japanese Names   135

Acknowledgments   139

Contributors   141

Foreword
Dōgen in the Twenty-first Century

The world is becoming more and more embroiled in complexity and confusion. Although the East-West confrontational structure that was the main cause of the cold war has collapsed, we do not have a new springtime of hope for the world. Instead, our situation appears to be more serious than ever and people everywhere nurse deep anxieties about the future. We face countless problems, including racial and ethnic conflicts, environmental crises, disappearing natural resources, and the deep-seated problem of human rights. We had hoped to create a bright future with civilizations built on science and technology, but we now find ourselves questioning the values of that civilization in a very fundamental way.

All our problems, whether they have to do with wars, the environment, or human rights, arise from human beings. To solve these terrible problems of the modern world we need to mobilize the combined strengths of government, economics, philosophy, science, and technology, but we also need to bear in mind that it is the human being, the self, that holds the key to transformation.

Any serious attempt to face the problems of our world requires as a first step that we rigorously examine ourselves. Eihei Dōgen, the great Japanese Zen master, was born eight hundred years ago, but his teachings are still fresh and clear today because he addressed the essential, unchanging human condition. He espoused the Buddha Way—a path of wholehearted living and of acceptance of our true nature—as a direction anyone can walk from wherever they start. If we want to understand life and perhaps to follow this Way, we have to begin by studying ourselves. Dōgen said, "To study the Buddha Way is to study the self; to study the self is to forget the self."

He taught that zazen, or seated meditation, is a prime way to accomplish this study of the self and to see deeply into the world. In zazen our differences drop away, and there we will find the truth attested to by all living and inanimate beings. Only in such a state can we convincingly appeal to the world with the idea that all problems consist in the excessive desire and attachment of each individual human being. Only in this state are we able to concentrate on methods of practice such as the six perfections—giving, morality, patience, vigor, meditation and wisdom.

Where, then, can we find the energy to study the self? Dōgen tells us that it is found in the mind that yearns for the ancient way of the buddhas and ancestors and that this is nothing other than the mind that saves all people. In accordance with the mind that yearns for the ancient way of the buddhas and ancestors, we can live our lives practicing zazen, investigating the self and confronting the sufferings of the world.

Dōgen's message for the twenty-first century can be summed up in three principles: first, the way to understand life and its problems lies in studying the self; second, the life of the individual human being is Buddha's life; and third, nature is the expression and life of buddha, or awakening.

These three principles can point us toward three parallel lines of action for our involvement with the problems of the world: first, as a basis for spiritual insight, disseminate the teaching that to study the Buddha Way is to study the self, and to study the self is to forget the self; second, to meet the problems of peace, human rights, ethnicity, and ethics, investigate the meaning of "birth and death are the very life of the Buddha"; and third, grapple with environmental problems, believing that at this moment mountains and rivers manifest the way of the ancient buddhas.

Because of his timeless and encompassing approach, Dōgen's writings are as relevant today as they were in the thirteenth century. This book is an important, classic study of how to live a life of great and wide meaning in every simple daily activity. *Instructions for the Cook* are instructions for life. The essays following the translation are individual responses to Dōgen's *Instructions* by modern masters who are his descendants, people for whom Dōgen is himself the ancient buddha, and for whom the path he shows is the ancient path for which they yearn. I hope they will be able to guide you to see what their eyes see, so that you may see your own way that much clearer.

> Ekiho Miyazaki
> *Abbot of Eiheiji*
> *Head Monastery of the Sōtō School in Japan*
> *Founded by Zen Master Eihei Dōgen in 1244*

Introduction
Sharing Dōgen's World

Dōgen, born in the year 1200, grew up in a world very different from ours. His father, who died when his son was scarcely out of infancy, was a member of the old aristocratic Minamoto family descending from Emperor Murakami (946–67). His mother, also from an aristocratic family, died when he was just eight years old. Only a few years later Dōgen cut short his training for a civil service career and fled to the monastic world, where he entered a strictly hierarchical realm of arcane learning and devotions. While still in his twenties, unsatisfied with what he could learn in Japan, he undertook the dangerous voyage to Song-dynasty China—yet another world very different from our own—where he was confronted with a style of religious practice that challenged the very foundation of his being. *Instructions for the Cook* is the record of that challenge and of Dōgen's response. It is his expression of the emphasis in Zen on maintaining spiritual cultivation in every moment of one's life, interpreted for his Japanese contemporaries.

It is well to bear in mind how radically different Dōgen's origins, upbringing, and religious training were from our own. Today, for example, it is nothing special to hop on a plane and fly to Shanghai, and thence travel to Nanjing and the very monasteries where Dōgen trained. In Dōgen's time the trip from Japan to China took weeks or months and was extremely risky. Very few made the journey. At the turn of the present century China is of course an imposing presence in the world, but its status today is nothing compared to what it was for

Dōgen and Japan in his day. Then the Middle Kingdom was truly the center of civilization itself, and overwhelmingly the source of Japan's culture.

China was effectively the origin of Japan's Buddhism too. The distant roots of the religion in India were remembered, and centuries before Dōgen's time a few Indian and Southeast Asian monks had found their way to the Japanese archipelago, but no Japanese pilgrim had ever made it there and back. Buddhism had first arrived from China and Korea in the sixth century, and by the thirteenth century it had already gone through a major cycle of expansion, institutionalization, and reform in Japan. In Dōgen's time those reformers had become the establishment in which he trained and which he then rejected.

While we might think that Zen has experienced a "boom" in America and the West in recent times, during the thirteenth century it was one of the dominant forms of religion in the largest and most vibrant civilization in the world. Newly arriving in Japan in the thirteenth century, Zen was welcomed eagerly, if not without contention, by the Japanese. Not only was it the latest and greatest thing from the continent, but its very newness made it susceptible to exploitation and control by the military authorities.

Dōgen's goal upon returning to Japan was to establish the practice of Buddhism according to the understanding he had achieved during his years of study in China. Although in hindsight he is called the founder of the Sōtō Zen school in Japan, he himself did not see things that way. He insisted throughout his writings that he was trying to present the original, primary teachings of Buddhism as handed on by generations of masters in India and China. He moved cautiously at first upon his return, staying at Kenninji, where he had practiced for some time before leaving for China, and then building up his own community at Kōshōji, just south of modern Kyoto. At the same time, he acted with an assurance unusual for such a young man. With the benefit of knowing what he was to achieve, we can appreciate his inner drive and the grandeur of his religious vision, but he may have impressed some of his contemporaries as arrogant. The results of Dōgen's initial efforts can only be described as mixed: he attracted a number of students but failed to win significant support from the most powerful figures in the land, who turned their attentions to other more recently returned Japanese Zen pilgrims to China, not to mention the earliest Chinese Chan (as Zen is called in China) missionaries themselves. Such backing was crucial to establishing a training center and a venue for teaching, and we can only imagine why

Dōgen lost this competition for support. Perhaps his major rival, a Rinzai Zen school priest, was a bit more polished, a bit more accommodating and politically adept; and certainly the Chinese missionaries had a cultural legitimacy Dōgen could never achieve.

The Sōtō tradition would have us believe that Dōgen was not really interested in receiving comparable attention, that he left for the mountain wilderness of Echizen and what was to become the Sōtō training center of Eiheiji out of respect for his teacher's advice to avoid the wealthy and powerful. But Dōgen chose to follow this advice so long after it had been tendered that we can easily recognize this to be a transparent rationalization. In the end, Dōgen's failure at the court became one of the major causes of his longlasting success: Sōtō Zen flourished in the countryside in ways that allowed it to survive the travails of the Sengoku, or Warring States, period of the fifteenth and sixteenth centuries, which swept away the court- and government-supported Gozan, or Five Mountains, the Zen establishment that had been erected through the efforts of generations of mostly Rinzai practitioners.

Instructions for the Cook was written to explain both to Dōgen's immediate students at Kōshōji and to the Japanese world at large how true religious practice should be undertaken. It was completed relatively soon after his return from China, when the direction of his life was still uncertain, at least in terms of the location and clientele of his teaching. As such, along with the *Bendōwa, Fukan Zazengi,* and *Genjō Kōan*, it is one of the most articulate statements of his overall understanding of Buddhism, and it differs from those magnificent texts in being his most concrete explanation of how the principles of zazen are to be extended to all of one's daily life. It is also the most basic guideline for those who have decided to leave the householder's life and undertake full-time practice within the context of a monastic community.

This book includes a new translation of *Instructions for the Cook* by Professor Griffith Foulk, together with English renderings of Japanese essays on the text by commentators from the monastic and academic realms of modern Sōtō Zen. The translation of the text itself has been made possible through a new initiative to translate all of Dōgen's writings sponsored by the Sōtō School. Given the precise and eloquent articulation of Dōgen's original message in Foulk's English version, we are certain that readers will be richly rewarded for delving into this important primary scripture, one of the true classics of East Asian Buddhism.

The essays presented here alongside Foulk's translation represent a new and different type of offering to English readers, for here we have made available sources for understanding how Japanese priests and teachers working in recent decades have understood Dōgen's significance. Previous writings on the Zen tradition have included translations and studies of primary documents, sometimes with line-by-line commentary by the translator or a Zen teacher. As far as we know, however, this is the first time English readers have been given direct access to the way a broad spectrum of contemporary Japanese authorities on Zen have interpreted one of the classics of their own tradition.

This means, of course, that the origins of this book are even more complex than the opening comparison between Dōgen's life and our own. He was speaking to his contemporaries, perhaps with some hope but certainly with little assurance that his words might survive to be studied some seven or eight centuries later. Our Japanese essayists were writing for their own contemporaries as well. No doubt all of them were aware of the great interest in Zen among non-Japanese, and some of them may have recognized the profound impact that outsider interest had on the prominence and interpretation of Zen within Japan. But all this is speculation. They were writing for a Japanese audience, and although our current effort is in some sense continuous with theirs, having the support of the Sōtō school, they were not working to meet the needs of an English-language readership.

The title *Nothing Is Hidden* comes from a key incident in Dōgen's encounter with a Chinese monk in charge of a monastery kitchen, from whom he learned about practice that extends throughout all one's tasks. When they meet for the first time, the monk chastens Dōgen, telling him he doesn't yet understand what practice is. They meet again later and Dōgen has a chance to inquire further and asks, "What is wholehearted engagement of the way?" The monk answers, "In the whole world, it can never be hidden."

Part I presents Foulk's translation of Dōgen's original text and a short guide to it by a former abbot of Eiheiji, Renpō Niwa (all names are given in Western style, family name last; the custom in Japan puts the family name first).

In Parts II and III other masters offer personal views of Dōgen's *Instructions*, sharing its meaning for their own lives: Shundō Aoyama, Dainin Katagiri, Zengan Hashimoto, Kōryō Shinno, and Kōshō Uchiyama. There are also essays by scholars—Kōdō Kurebayashi, Kōgen Mizuno, and Hisao Shinohara—addressing a broad audience.

Considering that the original book was created solely for a Japanese audience, it is perhaps surprising that no fewer than three of these masters have taken an active personal interest in the transmission of Zen to the West. Aoyama Roshi, the sole woman author, leads a training center for women priests where a handful of Westerners have trained, and she has twice visited and lectured in the United States. Katagiri Roshi founded the Minnesota Zen Meditation Center and taught in the United States for twenty-five years. He was the only author asked to write for the book while teaching in the West. Uchiyama Roshi encouraged many Westerners who studied with him at his nontraditional training center, and he urged his disciples to go to the West; one of them is Shōhaku Okumura, one of the primary translator-editors of this project. Their teachings in this volume, like those of the others, are both universal in scope and deeply grounded in their own particular lives.

The essays presented here were originally published by Eiheiji in 1978 under the title *Tenzo Kyōkun no Sankyū (Examination of Instructions for the Cook)*. The book was reissued in Japan by a commercial press in Tokyo (Kokusho Kankō Kai) as part of the commemorative events for the eight hundredth anniversary of Dōgen's birth and the seven hundred fiftieth anniversary of his death.

The proximate origins of this volume go back to work in the fall of 1997 by Eiheiji's committee on international commemorative events for the Dōgen anniversary. In a brainstorming meeting in Los Angeles organized to develop ideas for events to be held in the United States, two projects were proposed: a Dōgen symposium, which was held at Stanford University in the fall of 1999, and this translation project. The record of the symposium, including all the presentations, will be published by the Administrative Headquarters of the Sōtō School (Shūmuchō) in Japan.

There are many places where the translators and editors of these essays have chosen to abbreviate, modify, and even supplement the texts. In this case translating has meshed so closely with editing as almost to merge, heightening the refrain that runs through translators' minds, "All translation is interpretation." We hope we have reached a creative tension between the pull toward adhering so closely to the original that clarity and readability are sacrificed, and the pull toward putting it so far into colloquial English that its roots in individual, Japanese, lives and experience are lost.

Foulk's translation uses the word "cook" and tells you at length just what sort of cook this is. Lacking this extensive kind of explanation, the essays use "tenzo" instead, as a shorthand to indicate one who prepares meals as an expression of wholehearted practice of the Buddha Way and as the generous offering of one's life efforts on others' behalf, whether in a monastery or a diner.

Let us add one final word before sending the reader on to a direct encounter with Dōgen's masterpiece and some of its outstanding modern interpretations. We began by remarking on the social privilege Dōgen enjoyed at the beginning of his life. You, the reader, share in a different sort of privilege in the opportunity to meet his religious genius and its modern commentary. We may all live in widely separate contexts, separated from each other by vast realms of time, space, and culture, but the medium of the written word serves to bring us all together. If we can reach across the centuries and the seas simply by reading, we can work to include other worldviews, and other inspirations, in our own. Perhaps the world we live in is not so very different from Dōgen's after all.

> John McRae, *Indiana University*
> Jisho Warner, *Stone Creek Zendo*
> Shōhaku Okumura, *Sōtō Zen Education Center*
> Taigen Dan Leighton, *San Francisco Zen Center*

PART I

Dōgen's Instructions for the Cook

Instructions for the Cook

translated by Griffith Foulk

By the monk Dōgen of the Kannon Dōri Kōshō Hōrin Zen Monastery

Buddhist monasteries have, in principle, six stewards.[1] All are disciples of Buddha and all carry out the work of Buddha. Among them is the officer known as the cook, who is in charge of preparing meals for the assembly of monks. The *Rules of Purity for Chan Monasteries* (*Chanyuan Qinggui*) says, "In order to offer nourishment to the monks of the community, there is a cook."[2] From ancient times, the position has been assigned to senior monks who have the way-seeking mind, to eminent persons who have aroused the thought of awakening.

In general, the job of cook is an all-consuming engagement of the way. If one lacks the way-seeking mind, it will be nothing but a vain struggle and hardship, without benefit in the end. The *Rules of Purity for Chan Monasteries* says, "One should maintain a way-seeking mind, make adjustments in accord with the occasion, and see to it that the great assembly receives what is necessary and is at ease."[3] In days of yore, monks such as Guishan and Dongshan performed this job,[4] and various other great ancestral teachers did too at some point in their careers. Thus, it is surely not the same as the work of worldly cooks, imperial chefs, and the like.

When this mountain monk [I, Dōgen] was in Song China, on my days off I inquired of retired elderly monks who had held minor and important offices, and they shared something of their views with me. Their explanations are the bones and marrow bequeathed by the buddhas and ancestors who were possessed of the way in ancient times.[5] As a rule, one should carefully read the *Rules of Purity for Chan Monasteries*. After that, one should pay heed to the detailed explanations of those retired senior officers.

The duties of the cook over the course of a single day and night [are as follows].

First, following the midday meal, go to the offices of the prior and comptroller and get the ingredients for the next day's meals: rice, vegetables, and so on. Having received them, protect and be frugal with them, as if they were your own eyes. Chan Master Yong of Baoning [Monastery] said,[6] "Protect and be frugal with monastery property, which is [like] your own eyes." Respect and value them as if they were ingredients for an imperial repast. These cautions apply to fresh and cooked things alike.

Next, the various stewards consult in the store hall about what seasonings should be used on the following day, what vegetables should be eaten, how the rice gruel should be prepared, and so on. The *Rules of Purity for Chan Monasteries* says, "When deciding about ingredients as well as the flavors and numbers [of side dishes] for meals, first consult with the stewards in the store offices."[7] The stewards referred to here are the prior, comptroller, assistant comptroller, monks' supervisor, cook, and labor steward.[8] When the flavors and numbers have been decided, write them on the announcement boards in the abbot's quarters, common quarters, and elsewhere.

After that, ready the next morning's rice gruel. When washing rice, preparing vegetables, and so on, do so with your own hands, with close attention, vigorous exertion, and a sincere mind. Do not indulge in a single moment of carelessness or laziness. Do not allow attentiveness to one thing to result in overlooking another. Do not yield a single drop in the ocean of merit; even a mountain of good karma can be augmented by a single particle of dust.

The *Rules of Purity for Chan Monasteries* says, "If the six flavors are not refined and the three virtues are not provided, then it cannot be said that the cook has served the assembly."[9] When examining the rice, first check for sand; when examining the sand [sifted from the rice], first check for rice. If you pay careful attention to detail, watching when coming and watching when going, then your mind cannot be scattered, and [the food] will naturally be replete with the three virtues and endowed with the six flavors.

When Xuefeng resided at Dongshan [Monastery], he served as cook.[10] One day when he was sifting rice [Master] Dongshan asked him, "Are you sifting the sand and removing the rice, or sifting the rice and removing the sand?"[11] Xuefeng said, "Sand and rice are simultaneously removed." Dongshan asked, "What will the great assembly eat?" Xuefeng overturned the bowl. Dongshan said, "In the future you will go and be scrutinized by someone else."

In the past, eminent men in possession of the way practiced in this way [as cooks], working energetically with their own hands. In this latter day, how can we who are so late getting started [in our practice] be negligent about this? The ancients said that cooks regard tying up their sleeves [for manual work] as the way-seeking mind. Lest there be any mistakes in the sifting out of rice and sand, you should examine it with your own hands. The *Rules of Purity* say, "When preparing meals, one should reflect intimately on one's own self; [the food] will then of itself be pure and refined."[12]

Keep the white water with which you have washed the rice; do not wastefully discard it. In ancient times they used a cloth bag to strain the white water and used it to boil the rice when making gruel. Having put [the rice] into the cooking pot, pay attention and guard it. Do not allow mice and the like to touch it by mistake, nor any desirous idlers to examine or touch it.

When cooking the vegetable side dishes for the morning gruel, also prepare the platters and tubs used for rice, soup, and so forth, as well as the various utensils and supplies that will be used for that day's midday meal. Wash them so that they are completely pure and clean, placing up high those that belong in high places, and putting down low those that belong in low places. "High places are high and level; low places are low and level."[13] Treat utensils such as tongs and ladles, and all other implements and ingredients, with equal respect; handle all things with sincerity, picking them up and putting them down with courtesy.

When you have finished, think about the ingredients for the next day's meals. First, pick over the rice. If there are any insects, raw beans, hulls or pebbles, carefully pick them out. While picking over the rice and vegetables, the postulant should chant sutras and dedicate the merit to the kitchen god. Next, select the ingredients for the vegetables and soup and cook them. Do not argue with the store officers over the amount of ingredients you have received.[14] Without worrying about their quality, simply make the best of what you have. It is prohibited to show your feelings or say anything about the amount of ingredients.

During the day and through the night, whether things come and dwell in your mind or your mind turns and dwells on things, put yourself on a par with them and diligently engage the way. Prior to the third watch take stock of the next morning's tasks; after the third watch take charge of making the morning gruel. When that day's gruel is finished, wash the pots, steam the rice, and prepare the soup. When soaking the rice for the midday meal, the cook should not leave the vicinity of the sink. Keep a sharp eye on everything, so as not to waste even a single grain, and properly rinse out any foreign objects. Put the rice in the pots, light the fires, and steam it. Of old it was said, "When steaming rice, treat the pot as your own head; when rinsing the rice, know that the water is your own lifeblood." When the steaming is done, collect the rice in a bamboo basket or rice tub and place it on the table. Preparation of vegetables, soup, and the like should be done while the rice is being steamed.

The cook keeps careful watch over the area where the rice and soup are prepared, giving commands to the postulants, the servants, and the fire stokers and instructing them in the handling of the various utensils. Nowadays large monasteries have rice cooks and soup cooks, but those nevertheless are under the command of the cook. In the past there were no such rice or soup cooks, only the single officer, the cook himself.

When ordinarily preparing ingredients, do not regard them with ordinary [deluded] eyes, or think of them with ordinary emotions. "Lifting a single blade of grass builds a buddha land;[15] entering a single mote of dust turns the great wheel of the dharma."[16] Even when, for example, one makes a soup of the crudest greens, one should not give rise to a mind that loathes it or takes it lightly; and even when one makes a soup of the finest cream,[17] one should not give rise to a mind that feels glad and rejoices in it. If one is at the outset free from preferences, how could one have any aversions? Even when confronted with poor ingredients, there is no negligence whatsoever; even when faced with scanty ingredients, one exerts oneself. Do not change your mind in accordance with things. Whoever changes his mind in accordance with things, or revises his words to suit the person [he is speaking to], is not a man of the way.

With resolve and sincerity, one should aim to exceed the ancients in purity and to surpass the former worthies in attentiveness. The way to put that aspiration into practice in one's own person is, for example, to take the same three coins that one's predecessors spent to make a soup of the crudest greens and to use them now to make a soup of the finest cream. This is difficult to do. Why is that? Because present and past are completely different, like the distance between heaven and earth. How could we ever be able to equal their stature? Nevertheless, when we work attentively, therein lies the principle that makes it possible to surpass our predecessors.

That you still do not grasp the certainty of this principle is because your thinking scatters, like wild horses, and your emotions run wild, like monkeys in a forest.[18] If you can make those monkeys and horses, just once, take the backward step that turns the light and shines it inward, then naturally you will be completely integrated. This is the means by which we, who are [ordinarily] set into motion by things, become able to set things into motion.

Harmonizing and purifying yourself in this manner, do not lose either the one eye [of transcendent wisdom] or the two eyes [of discriminating consciousness]. Lifting a single piece of vegetable, make [yourself into] a six-foot body [i.e. a buddha] and ask that six-foot body to prepare a single piece of vegetable. Those are [the cook's] spiritual penetrations and magical transformations; his buddha-work and benefiting of living beings.

When you have prepared, the preparations are completed. When you have cooked, the cooking is attained. Then you should look to "that side" and put away things on "this side."[19] When the drum sounds or the bell rings, join the assembly [of monks in training] and attend the convocation [to hear the abbot's teachings]. "Morning and evening, seek and attend,"[20] without being remiss even once.

When you return to your quarters, right away you should close your eyes and clearly envision the number of individual places in the [sangha] hall; the number of monks in the individual quarters of retired minor officers, retired senior officers, and the like; how many individual monks there are in the infirmary, geriatric quarters, temporaries' quarters, and so on; the number of wandering monks registered in the guest quarters; and the number of people in subtemples. After carefully calculating in this way, if you have the slightest uncertainty, ask the hall manager in question, or the prefects, chiefs, or head seats of the various quarters and eliminate your doubts.

Now carefully calculate: for every grain of rice to be eaten, one grain must be supplied. If a single grain of rice is divided, then you will have two half-grains of rice. Three-tenths, four-tenths; one-half, two halves. If you supply two half-grains of rice, you will make a single whole grain. Or, supply nine-tenths and see how many tenths you still have; now take back nine-tenths and see how many tenths are still there.

Getting to eat a single grain of Luling rice enables one to see the monk Guishan;[21] getting to supply a single grain of Luling rice enables one to see the water buffalo [that Guishan will become]. The water buffalo eats the monk Guishan, and the monk Guishan feeds the buffalo. Is my measurement complete or not? Is your calculation complete or not? If you carefully inspect and exhaustively check [these matters], your understanding will dawn and become clear. Then, when an opportunity presents itself, say something; when you confront someone, speak. And, if you exert yourself in this way without deviation, day after day, then you will not be able to forget it, even temporarily.

When a patron comes into the monastery and donates money to hold a feast, the various stewards should all be consulted; this is the precedent established in monasteries of old. With regard to the distribution of the merit-making donations, they also consult together. Do not create a disturbance in the hierarchy by infringing on anyone's authority.

When the midday meal or morning gruel has been properly prepared and placed on the table, the cook dons his kesa, spreads his sitting cloth, faces the sangha hall [where the monks eat], burns incense, and makes nine prostrations. Upon finishing his prostrations, he sends the food [to the sangha hall].

Throughout the day, as you prepare the meals, do not pass the time in vain. If your preparations are true, then your movements and activities will naturally become the deeds of nurturing the womb of the sage. The way to put the great assembly at ease is to step back and transform yourself.

It has been a long time now since the name "buddha dharma" came to be heard in our country, Japan. However, our predecessors did not record, and the former worthies did not teach, anything about the proper procedure for monks' meals, and they never even dreamed of the rite of making nine prostrations before the monks' meals. Our countrymen say that the way monks eat and the way monasteries prepare food are no better than the feeding of [domestic] birds and beasts. This is truly pathetic, truly deplorable. How could it be?

When this mountain monk [I, Dōgen] was at Tiantong Monastery, the position [of cook] was held by Cook Yong, of the same province [as the monastery]. Once, after the midday meal I was passing through the east corridor on my way to the Chaoran room [where my teacher Myōzen was being nursed] when I saw the cook in front of the buddha hall airing mushrooms. He carried a bamboo staff in his hand, but had no hat on his head. The sun was hot, the ground tiles were hot, and sweat streamed over him as he worked diligently to dry the mushrooms. He was suffering a bit. With his backbone bent like a bow and his shaggy eyebrows, he resembled a crane.

I approached and asked the cook his dharma age. He said, "Sixty-eight years." I said, "Why do you not employ lay trainees or laborers?" He said, "They are not me." I said, "Venerable sir, your attitude is indeed proper, but the sun is so hot; why are you doing this [now]?" The cook said, "What time should I wait for?" I took my leave, but as I walked along the corridor, I began to realize how important an opportunity this position affords.

Again, in the fifth month of the sixteenth year of the Jiading era [1223], I was on the ship at Qingyuan. While I was talking with the Japanese captain, an old monk arrived. He was about sixty years old. He came directly onto the ship and inquired of the Japanese passengers if he could buy Japanese mushrooms. I invited him to drink tea and asked where he was from. He was the cook of the monastery on Mount Ayuwang. He said, "I come from Sichuan, but I left my home village forty years ago. This year I am sixty-one years old. In the past I have trained in quite a few different monasteries. In recent years, I stayed for a while with Guyun. I was able to register at Yuwang [Monastery], but for some time I felt out of place. At the end of the summer retreat last year, however, I was appointed cook of that monastery. Tomorrow is the fifth day [feast], but the entire menu does not yet include a single delicacy. I need to cook noodle soup, but still have no mushrooms, and thus have made a special trip here to try to buy mushrooms to offer to the monks of the ten directions."

I asked him, "What time did you leave there?" The cook replied, "After the midday meal." I inquired, "How long is the road from Yuwang to here?" He said, "Thirty-four or thirty-five li."[22] I asked, "When will you return to the monastery?" He said, "If I can buy the mushrooms now, I will set off right after that." I said, "Today I did not expect to meet you and have a conversation on this ship. It is most fortunate, is it not, to form this karmic bond? Dōgen [I] will treat the cook Zen master [you] to a meal." The cook said, "It is impossible. If I do not oversee the preparations for tomorrow's meal offering, it will not turn out well." I said, "Are there not coworkers in the monastery who understand the meals? What will be deficient if only one officer, the cook, is not present?" The cook said, "I took up this position in my later years; it is this old man's engagement of the way. How could I hand it over to others? Besides, when I came I did not ask to stay away overnight."

I again asked the cook: "You are venerable in years; why don't you sit in meditation to engage the way or contemplate the words of the ancients? It is troublesome being cook; all you do is labor. What good is that?" The cook laughed and said, "My good man from a foreign country, you do not yet understand engagement of the way and do not yet know about words." When I heard him speak in this manner, I suddenly felt ashamed and taken aback. I asked him, "What are words? What is the practice of the way?" The cook said, "If you do not slip up and pass by the place you ask about, how could you not be a man?" At the time, I did not understand. The cook said, "If you still don't understand, come to Yuwang Mountain at some other time, in the future. On that occasion we can discuss the principle of words." Having spoken thus, the cook got up and said, "It is late in the day and I am in a hurry, so I am going back now."

In the seventh month of the same year, I registered at Tiantong [Monastery]. While I was there, that cook came to meet me and said, "At the end of the summer retreat I retired as cook and am now returning to my home village. I happened to hear a disciple say that you were here; how could I not come to meet you?"

I jumped for joy and was very grateful. In the ensuing conversation that I had with him I brought up the karmic conditions of words and engagement of the way that we had discussed previously on the ship. The cook said, "The study of words is to understand the purpose of words. Exertion in engagement of the way requires an affirmation of the purpose of engaging the way." I asked him, "What are words?" The cook answered, "One, two, three, four, five." I also asked, "What is engagement of the way?" He said, "In the whole world, it can never be hidden."

Although we discussed a great variety of other things, I will not record them at this point. The little I know about words and understand about engaging the way is due to the great kindness of that cook. I told my late teacher Myōzen about the things that I have just related here, and he was very happy to hear of them.

Later I saw a verse that Xuedou wrote to instruct the monks:[23]

One letter, seven letters, three letters, or five;
Investigating myriads of images, one reaches no basis.
In the depth of night, the moon sets into the dark sea;
Seeking the black dragon's pearl, one finds there are many.

What that cook said some years before and what Xuedou expresses in this verse clearly coincide. More and more I understand that the cook was a true man of the way. But in the past what I saw of written words was one, two, three, four, five. Today what I see of written words is also six, seven, eight, nine, ten.

You disciples who come after me, thoroughly contemplate there in accordance with here and thoroughly contemplate here in accordance with there. If you make this kind of effort you will be able to obtain in words the Zen of a single flavor. If you are not like this, you will be subjected willy-nilly to the poison of the Zen of five flavors, and when it comes to arranging the monks' meals, you will not be able to do it skillfully.

I have heard of former cooks and witnessed present ones, with my eyes and with my ears. Concerning this position, there are words and there are principles of behavior; truly, it can be called a central one! Even if one has the title of abbot, one's mental attitude should still be the same as this. The *Rules of Purity for Chan Monasteries* says,

> The preparation of gruel and rice for the two daily meals should be refined and plentiful. The provision of the four types of offerings must not admit to any lack or scarcity. The World-honored One bequeathed the blessings of twenty years to enfold his descendants.[24] The merit of a single beam of white light [emitted from his forehead], when received and used [by his descendants] is never exhausted. Therefore, just know that in serving the assembly, there can be no fear of scarcity.[25]

If you do not have a mind that is limited, as a matter of course there will be no lack of blessings. After all, this is the mental attitude that the abbot has in providing for the assembly.

As for the [proper] attitude in preparing food offerings and handling ingredients, do not debate the fineness of things and do not debate their coarseness, but take as essential the profound arousal of a true mind and a respectful mind.

Have you not seen that a single bowl of starchy water, offered to Him of the Ten Names, naturally resulted in wondrous merit that carried an old woman through future births;[26] and that half a crab apple fruit, given to a single monastery, enabled King Ashoka to finally establish his vast good karmic roots, gain a prediction, and bring about a great result?[27] Although they create a karmic connection with Buddha, [donations that are] large and vacuous are not the same as [ones that are] small and sincere. This is the practice of a [true] person.

What is regarded as the preparation of superb delicacies is not necessarily superior, nor is the preparation of a soup of the crudest greens necessarily inferior. When you select and serve up crude greens, if you do so with a true mind, a sincere mind, and a pure mind, then they will be comparable to superb delicacies. Why is that so? Because when one enters into the pure and vast oceanic assembly of the buddha dharma, superb delicacies are never seen and the flavor of crude greens does not exist: there is only the one taste of the great sea, and that is all. Moreover, when it comes to the matters of nurturing the sprouts of the way and nourishing the embryo of buddhahood, superb delicacies and crude greens are as one; there is no duality.[28] There is an old saying that a monk's mouth is like a stove.[29] You must not fail to understand this. You should think that even crude greens can nourish the sacred embryo and nurture the sprouts of the way. Do not regard them as base; do not take them lightly. The teacher of humans and devas is able to regard crude greens as things that convert and benefit [beings].

Moreover, you should not concern yourself with the strengths and weaknesses of the monks of the assembly, or look upon them as being old or young. Even the self does not know the self's own weak points; how could others be aware of the weak points of others? How could it not be a mistake to take one's own deficiencies as the deficiencies of others?

Although there are differences in the appearance of seniors and juniors, and some have wisdom while others are foolish or dim, as members of the sangha they are the same. Moreover, something that was not true in the past may be true at present, so who can know which are sages and which are commoners? The *Rules of Purity for Chan Monasteries* says, "The sangha gathers together from throughout the ten directions, without distinguishing sages and commoners."[30] If you have an aspiration that does not try to control all matters of right and wrong, is that not the way of practice that directly approaches supreme awakening? If you are confused about the step you have just taken, then you will slip up and pass by that which stares you in the face. The bones and marrow of the ancients consist entirely in the making of this kind of effort. Disciples in these later generations who hold the position of cook will also first attain [the bones and marrow] through this kind of effort. How could the rules of the high patriarch Baizhang be in vain?[31]

After I returned to Japan I took up residence in Kennin Monastery for several years. That monastery established the position of cook, but it was in name only; there was no one at all who actually carried it out. As yet unaware that this is the work of Buddha, how pathetic was their pursuit and practice of the way! Truly it is pitiable that they, without meeting such a person, vainly passed the days and recklessly destroyed the way of practice. Once I observed that the monk who held the position of cook at that monastery did nothing at all to manage the two daily meals. He entrusted all matters large and small to a servant without a brain or human feelings, giving him only general instructions. He never ever went to see whether the work was done properly or not. He acted just like a housewife, who would never go and look at her neighbor's home for fear of causing embarassment or insult. He ensconced himself in his office, sometimes reclining, sometimes chatting and laughing, sometimes reading sutras, and sometimes reciting prayers. For days on end and many months he did not approach the vicinity of the pots; how much less did he take stock of the utensils or pay attention to the flavors and numbers [of side dishes]. How could he possibly have done his job? Needless to say, he had never even dreamed of the two [daily] occasions for making nine prostrations. When the time came for instructing young lay trainees he never knew what to do. How pitiable and how sad was that person who lacked the way-seeking mind. Not once did he come into contact with a companion who was possessed of the virtue of the way. Although he entered into the treasure mountain, he came away with empty hands. Although he reached the treasure ocean, he turned back with empty body. You should know that even if he never aroused the thought of enlightenment, if he had seen a single person who set a worthy example he would have attained that way in his practice. And even if he never saw a single person who set a worthy example, if his thought of enlightenment had been profound, he would have hit upon that way in his practice. But in actuality both were lacking, so there was no way for him to benefit.

As I observed in the various monasteries and temples of the Great Song Nation, the monks who held the positions of stewards and prefects, although they only served for one year, each embodied the three ways of upholding [the buddha-dharma]. During their time [in office] they made use of these [three ways], and in their vying for karmic connections they inspired these. [1] Even as you benefit others, concurrently there are ample benefits for yourself. [2] Elevate the monastery pulpit and renew its high standing. [3] Standing shoulder to shoulder and competing head to head, follow in the footsteps of esteemed forerunners. You should have a detailed knowledge of these matters. There are fools who look upon themselves as if they were someone else, and there are wise people who regard others as themselves.

An ancient said,

Two-thirds of one's days having swiftly passed,
Not a single aspect of the spirit dais has been polished;

Craving life, day after day goes by in distress;
If one does not turn one's head when called, what can be done?

You should know that if you have not met a wise teacher, you are liable to be carried away by your emotions. How pitiable the foolish son who left behind the family fortune handed down to him by his prominent father and vainly labored in front of others handling garbage and excrement.[32] At present, are we not liable to be like this?

When I observed accomplished people in the past who held the position of cook, their personal qualities were naturally in accord with their official roles. The Great Gui awakened to the way when he was a cook.[33] Dongshan's [saying] "Three pounds of hemp" was also uttered when he was a cook.[34] If there is a matter that can be valued, you should value the matter of awakening to the way. If there is a time that can be valued, surely you should value the time of awakening to the way! The result of cherishing that matter and being addicted to the way is attested especially by the [story of] "grasping sand and making a jewel."[35] We can often see the effect of making an image [of Buddha] and worshiping [before it].[36] The position of cook is similar [in its karmic results], but even more so. Its name is the same [as in the past]. If the cook is someone who can transmit its character and its practice, how could its beauty and its fulfillment fail to appear?

In general, the various stewards and prefects, including the cook, should maintain a joyful mind, an elder's mind, and a great mind whenever they perform rituals or engage in work.

So-called joyful mind is the spirit of happiness. You should think that if you were born in a heaven, you would be attached to pleasures without cease and would not be able to arouse the thought of enlightenment; practice would not be feasible. Even less would you be able to prepare meals as offerings of the three jewels! Among the myriad dharmas, the most revered and precious are the three jewels. The most superior things are the three jewels. Indra cannot compare. A wheel-turning king does not equal them. The *Rules of Purity* says, "Revered by the world, it is an excellent space outside [worldly] things; pure and detached, the assembly of monks is best."[37] Now we have the good fortune to be born as human beings and to prepare the food that these three jewels receive and use. Is this not of great karmic significance? We should thus be very happy.

Again, you should think that if you were born into the realms of hell, hungry ghosts, animals, demigods, and the like, or born in circumstances where you suffered from one of the eight difficulties, even if you sought to cloak yourself in the power of the sangha, your hands would naturally be unable to prepare pure meals as offerings to the three jewels. Relying on that painful physical form you would receive pain and be bound in body and mind. Now, in this life, you have already prepared those meals. How happy a birth! How happy a body! It is the good karmic result of kalpas vast and great. It is merit that cannot decay. When you prepare food and cook it you should do so with the aspiration of taking tens of thousands of births and concentrating them into this one day, this one time, that you may be able to bind together in good karmic result the bodies of millions of [past] births. A mind that contemplates and understands things in this way is a joyful mind. Truly, even if one takes on the body of a wheel-turning holy king, if one does not prepare meals as offerings to the three jewels, in the end it has no benefit. It is only of the nature of water, froth, bubbles, or flames.

Elder's mind is the spirit of fathers and mothers. It is, for example, like a father and mother who dote on an only child: one's thoughts of the three jewels are like their concentration on that one child. Even if they are poor or desperate, they strongly love and nurture that single child. People who are outsiders cannot understand their state of mind; they can only understand it when they become fathers or mothers. Without regard for their own poverty or wealth, [parents] earnestly turn their thoughts toward raising their child. Without regard for whether they themselves are cold or hot, they shade the child or cover the child. We may regard this as affection at its most intense. A person who arouses this spirit is fully conscious of it. A person who cultivates this spirit is one who truly awakens to it. Therefore, when [the cook] watches over water and watches over grain, in every case he should sustain the caring and warmth of child-rearing!

The great teacher Shakyamuni, moreover, apportioned twenty years of his lifespan as a buddha to assist us in this age of the end of the dharma. What was his intention? It was simply that he valued the spirit of fathers and mothers. A Tathagata is utterly incapable of seeking any reward or seeking any riches.

Great mind is, in its spirit, like a great mountain or a great sea: it has no partiality and no factionalism. Lifting an ounce, it does not consider it light; hefting a stone, it does not consider it heavy.[38] Being drawn by the voices of spring, it does not wander into the swamp of spring. Although it sees the colors of autumn, it has nothing whatsoever of the spirit of autumn. It contrasts the four seasons against the backdrop of a single vista. It views pennyweights and ounces [of silver] within the context of a single system of measurement.[39] As an emblem of this sameness, we can write the character "great." You should know the character "great." You should study the character "great." If the cook of Jiashan [Monastery] had not studied the character "great," he would not have spontaneously laughed his single laugh, and would not have saved Taiyuan.[40]

If Zen Master Guishan had not written the character "great," he could not have taken a stick of firewood and blown on it three times.[41] If the Reverend Preceptor Dongshan had not known the character "great," he would not have been able to instruct the monk by raising "three pounds of hemp."[42] You should know that the great teachers of old were alike in their study of the character "great" in connection with the diverse phenomena of this world. Now, too, there are those who freely make a great sound, expound the great meaning, complete the great matter, connect with great people, and accomplish karmic conditions of this one great matter. How could abbots, stewards, prefects, and monks in training entirely forget these three kinds of mind?!

Recorded in the spring of the third year of the Katei era [1237] as instruction for accomplished practitioners of the way in the future.

Recorded by the dharma-transmitting monk Dōgen, abbot of the Kannon Dōri Kōshō Hōrin Zen Monastery.

■ ■ ■

1 The six stewards (*roku chiji*) are: prior (*tsūsu*), comptroller (*kansu*), assistant comptroller (*fūsu*), monks' supervisor or rector (*inō*), cook (*tenzo*), labor steward (*shissui*). There are also six prefects (*roku chōshu*): chief seat (*shuso*), scribe (*shoki*), sutra prefect (*zōsu*), guest prefect (*shika*), bath prefect (*chiyoku*), and Buddha Hall prefect (*chiden*).
2 The passage that Dōgen quotes may be found in Kagamishima Genryū, Sotō Tatsugen and Kosaka Kiyū, eds. and trans., *Yakuchū Zen'en Shingi* (Tokyo: Sōtōshū Shūmuchō, 1972), 269.
3 The passage that Dōgen quotes may be found in Kagamishima, et al., *Yakuchū Zen'en Shingi*, 116.
4 Guishan Lingyou (771–853); Dongshan Shouchu (910–90).
5 The expression "bones and marrow" is an allusion to a famous story in which Bodhidharma tests his four disciples. There were many variations, but the

version that Dōgen most likely knew was one found in the *Jingde Record* (*Jingde Chuandeng Lu*):

> After nine years had passed [since Bodhidharma's arrival in China], he wished to return to the west, to India, so he commanded his disciples saying, "The time is near; each of you should say what you have attained." At the time, the disciple Daofu replied, "As I see it, the function of the Dao consists in not attaching to scriptures and not being apart from scriptures." The master said, "You have gotten my skin." The nun Zongchi said, "My understanding now is that it is like the joy of seeing the Buddha-land of Akshobha: it is felt at the first glance, but not the second glance." The master said, "You have gotten my flesh." Daoyu said, "The four elements are at root empty, and the five skandhas have no existence; from my point of view, there is not a single dharma that could be attained." The master said, "You have gotten my bones." Finally Huike, after making a prostration, just stood at his place. The master said, "You have gotten my marrow" (T 51.219b27-c5).

6   Baoning Renyong (n.d.)
7   The passage that Dōgen quotes may be found in Kagamishima, et al., *Yakuchū Zen'en Shingi*, 116.
8   These are the so-called six stewards (roku chiji) mentioned above.
9   The passage that Dōgen quotes may be found in *Yakuchū Zen'en Shingi*, 273.
10 Xuefeng Yicun (822–908).
11 Dongshan Liangjie (807–69).
12 The passage that Dōgen quotes may be found in *Yakuchū Zen'en Shingi*, 116.
13 A famous saying taken from a dialogue between Guishan Lingyou (771–853) and his disciple Yangshan Huiji (807–83). As it appears in the *Jingde Era Record of the Transmission of the Flame* (*Jingde Chuandeng Lu*), the dialogue reads:

> One day [Yangshan] went along with Guishan to open a field. The teacher [Yangshan] asked, "Why is it that this part is low and that part is high?" Guishan said, "Water can level things; let us just water to level it." The teacher said, "Water is not reliable, master. It is just that high places are high and level; low places are low and level." Guishan assented (T51.282b18-21).

The dialogue appears in many other Zen texts, including: *Wujia Yulu* (*Dainippon Zokuzōkyō* 119.861a); (*Dainippon Zokuzōkyō* 118.66a); and Dōgen's *Eihei Kōroku* and *Sanbyaku Soku*. The saying "high places are high and level, low places are low and level" also appears in the *Foyan Chanshi Yulu* (*Dainippon Zokuzōkyō* 118-0515b13-14).

14 The store officers (*kusu*) are the six stewards (*roku chiji*), whose quarters and duties are in the storehouse.

15 This passage alludes to case 4 of the kōan collection *Congrong Record* (*Congronglu*), entitled "The World-honored One Points to the Ground" (*seson shichi*):

> When the World-honored One was walking with the assembly [of his followers], he pointed to the ground with his hand and said, "This place is suitable to build a shrine (*bonsetsu*)." [The deva] Indra took a single blade of grass, stuck it in the ground, and said, "I have built the shrine." The World-honored One smiled (T 48.230a3-5).

For a full translation of this case and its associated commentary, see Thomas Cleary, trans., *Book of Serenity: One Hundred Zen Dialogues* (Hudson, N.Y.: Lindisfarne Press, 1990), 17–19.

16 This passage alludes to a passage in fascicle 7 of the *Shurangama-samadhi Sutra* (*Shoulengyanjing*) which states :

> The tathagatas of the ten directions, embracing the spirit of this dharani, turn the great wheel of the dharma in lands [innumerable as] motes of dust (*Zengaku Daijiten*, 1182a, s.v. *mijin*).

17 Cream was not a common element in the Japanese diet in the thirteenth century, and it is doubtful that it would have been available to a cook in a Japanese Zen monatery at that time. Dogen, however, had trained in China, where the use of dairy products was more widespread, and he was writing in Chinese. Thus, whether he meant the reference to cream to be taken literally or just figuratively, it is not surprising that he should refer to it as a rare ingredient used to make the finest soup.

18 A more literal translation of this passage would be, "because your thinking flies in confusion like those wild horses." Taigen Dan Leighton and Shōhaku Okumura argue that the reference to "horses" in the popular edition is a mistake, and that the text originally has "birds," a noun that better matches the verb "to fly."

Instead of "birds," the common Rufubon edition has "horses." However, the earliest Kōshū version, copied by the fifteenth abbot Kōshū in the early sixteenth century, has "bird," which is clearly correct in the poetic context of the characters for the whole phrase (*Dōgen's Pure Standards for the Zen Community* [Albany: SUNY Press, 1996], 51, note 13).

The issue is not so clear, however. Andō Bun'ei notes that Dōgen was probably alluding to an "old saying" (*kogo*) that goes:

> *The mind monkey soars [through]*
> *The spreading branches of the desires*
> *The thought horse runs [through]*

The territory of the six senses.
(*Eihei Daishingi Tsūkai* [Tokyo: Kōmeisha, 1969], 44, note).

In this saying, monkeys soar (literally, "fly"—*tobi*); in the popular edition of *Tenzo Kyōkun*, horses scatter (literally, "fly in confusion"—*funbi*). In both cases, the "flying" is metaphorical and need not be taken literally as the action of birds.

19 A double entendre. On the literal level, the meaning is simply that the cook should look all around and put things away where they belong. Figuratively, he is advised to look "there" (*nahen*—the realm of the highest truth), while putting things to rest "here" (*shahen*—the worldly realm). Repetition of "preparations prepared" and "cooked cooking" is intentional and follows Dōgen's original.

20 A play on the common expression, "In the morning attend [the abbot's sermons] and in the evening seek [his instruction] (*chōsan boshō*)," which means to seek the dharma at all times.

21 Luling was a district in Jiangxi Province that produced a distinctive type of rice. The reference to Luling rice comes from a famous dialogue found in the biography of Chan master Qingyuan Xingsi (d. 740) in the *Jingde Era Record of the Transmission of the Flame* (*Jingdeng Lu*):

> A monk asked, "What is the ultimate meaning of the buddha dharma?"
> The master said, "What is the price of Luling rice?" (T51.240c2-3).

The same dialogue appears as case 5 in the *Congrong Record* (*Congrong Lu*; T 48.230a24-b24); for an English translation see Thomas Cleary, trans., *Book of Serenity: One Hundred Zen Dialogues* (Hudson, N.Y.: Lindisfarne Press, 1990), 20–22.

22 Li is a Chinese unit of distance equivalent to 1,890 feet, so 34 li are over 12 miles.

23 Xuedou Zhongsian (980–1052).

24 According to a subcommentary on the "Pure Practice" section of the *Avatamsaka Sutra* (*Huayanjing Jingxingpin Dashu*), the Buddha should have lived one hundred years, but he gave up his life at eighty in order to bequeath the remaining twenty years of merit to his followers in future generations.

25 The passage that Dōgen quotes may be found in *Yakuchū Zen'en Shingi*, 276.

26 The reference here is to the famous story of a poor old woman who made an offering to Buddha of the water that she had used to rinse rice and, as a result, was reborn as a deva or human for fifteen kalpas, gained a male body, and eventually became a buddha herself. The story appears in fascicle 8 of the *Treatise on the Great Perfection of Wisdom* (*Dazhidulun*).

27 King Ashoka, legend has it, tried to contribute a huge amount of gold to a monastery, but was prevented by his son and ministers. Next he tried to

donate his own gold eating utensils to the monastery, but was again thwarted. Finally he took half a crab apple that he had in his own hands and tried to offer that, but was unable to do so by himself. He enlisted the aid of another minister, who gave the fruit to the monks. They received it courteously, ground it into flour, and baked it into a cake, which was shared by all. This was Ashoka's final establishment of his good karmic roots. The story appears in fascicle 5 of the *Ashoka Sutra* (*Ayuwangjing*).

28 The term "embryo of buddhahood" or "sacred embryo" (*shōtai*) refers to the "embryo" of buddhahood in all beings that can be brought to maturity through practice.

29 A stove consumes all kinds of wood equally, regardless of its quality. A monk, similarly, should eat whatever is served without discriminating between plain and delicious.

30 The passage quoted appears in *Yakuchū Zen'en Shingi*, 276.

31 Baizhang (720–814) was the patriarch renowned in Song China as the founder of the first independent Chan monastery and author of the monastic rules. What Dōgen refers to as "Baizhang's rules," however, was none other than the *Rules of Purity for Chan Monasteries*, compiled in 1103.

32 This passage alludes to the famous parable of the "prodigal son" in the *Lotus Sutra* (*Fahuajing*). For an English translation see Leon Hurvitz, trans., *Scripture of the Lotus Blossom of the Fine Dharma* (New York: Columbia University Press, 1976), 85–95.

33 Guishan Lingyou (771–853).

34 The dialogue in which this reply occurs is a famous kōan, occurring as case 18 in the *Gateless Barrier* (*Wumenguan*) and case 12 in the *Blue Cliff Record* (*Biyanlu*). Leighton and Okumura suggest that the material referred to may not have been hemp (*ma*) but sesame (*zhima*) (*Dōgen's Pure Standards for the Zen Community*, 56, note 46).

35 A legend about King Ashoka relates how, as a boy in a former life, he was playing in the road with sand when the Buddha happened to pass by. The boy offered the sand to the Buddha as if it were dried grain. The Buddha accepted it and explained to his disciple Ananda that, one hundred years after his entry into nirvana, the boy would be a great wheel-turning king named Ashoka. The story appears in the "Birth Karma Chapter" (*Sheng Yinyuan Pinlü*) of the *Ashoka Sutra* (*Ayuwangjing*).

36 The effect that Dōgen is referring to is the karmic reward that results from performing a meritorious deed such as making a Buddha image or worshiping before one. Such effects are "often seen" in Buddhiist sutras and morality tales, which are filled with accounts of miraculous benefits (e.g. instant rescue from poverty, illness, injury, storms, wild animals, bad states of

rebirth, etc.) that come to people as a result of making and worshiping images or stupas.

37 The passage quoted appears in *Yakuchū Zen'en Shingi*, 270.

38 Dōgen was familiar with a Chinese system of weights in which 10 "bits" (Ch., *wen*; J., *mon*) equal one "ounce" or "tael" (Ch., *liang*; J., *ryō*) 16 "ounces" equal one "pound" or "catty" (Ch., *jin*; J. *kin*), and 30 "pounds" equal one "stone" (Ch., *jun*; J., *kin*). In the modern metric system, a "bit" is approximately 3.75 grams, an "ounce" is 37.5 grams, a "pound" is 600 grams, and a "stone" is 18 kilograms. "Great mind" is the subject referred to here as "it."

39 "Pennyweights" (Ch., *zhu*; J., *shu*) and "ounces" or taels (Ch., *liang*; J., *ryō*) were silver coins used in China when Dōgen was there. A one-ounce coin was equivalent in value to 24 pennyweight coins.

40 According to a story found in the *Collated Essentials of the Five Flame [Record]* (*Wudeng Buiyuan*) completed in 1253, the monk Taiyuan Fu (n.d.), also known as Elder Fu (Fu Shangzuo), was giving a lecture on the *Nirvana Sutra* (*Niepanjing*) at the Guangziao Monastery in Yangzhou. When he was explaining a reference to the dharma body (*fashen*) of the Buddha, a Chan monk (*chanzhe*) in the audience named Zuxue laughed. When the lecture was over Taiyuan invited him to drink tea and asked him why he had laughed. The Chan monk replied that he laughed because "the lecturer does not know the dharma body." Spurred by this criticism, Taiyuan sat in meditation in his room for ten days and eventually awakened when he heard a drum signaling the fifth watch of the night (*Zhonghua Shuju* 432.101-433.61). Taiyuan Fu is known as a disciple of Xuefeng Yicun (822–908).

Dōgen refers here to the monk who laughed as *Kassan no tenzo*, an ambiguous expression which may mean either "the cook of Jiashan [Monastery]" or "Jiashan the Cook." In the 59th chapter of his 95-chapter *Shōbōgenzō*, "Plum Flowers" (*Baika*), Dōgen also refers to the great awakening (*daigo*) of Elder Fu (Fu Jōza) as something stimulated by *Kassan no tenzo*, but here again the latter term is ambiguous. Leighton and Okumura translate *Kassan no tenzo* as "the tenzo of Jiashan Monastery" (*Dōgen's Pure Standards*, 49) and state in a note that his identity is otherwise unknown (Ibid., 57, note 55). Jiashan was a mountain in Hunan Province where Chan master Jiashan Shanhui (805–81), a dharma heir of Chuanzi Decheng (n.d.), built a meditation cloister in 870. It is possible that Dōgen thought of the monk whose laugh led to Taiyuan's awakening as an anonymous cook at Jiashan Monastery, but more likely his intention was to identify the monk as Jiashan himself, in his younger days as a cook. In his *Rules of Purity for Stewards* (*Chiji Shingi*), Dōgen cites a dialogue that took place between Chan master Guishan and Jiashan when the latter was serving as cook at Guishan Monastery (for an English translation, see Leighton and Okumura, *Dōgen's Pure Standards*, 141); the dialogue is also found in the *Discourse Records of the Five Houses* (*Wujia Yulu*), compiled in 1630. In his *Eihei Extensive Records* (*Eihei Kōroku*), s.v. "convocation to thank the cook" (*sha tenzo jōdō*), Dōgen names Jiashan, along with Wuzhe, Xuefeng, and others, as an exemplary cook of the past (0138). The *T'ien-sheng Era Extensive Record of the Flame* (*T'ien-sheng Kuang-teng Lu*), compiled in 1029, also mentions the name of "Jiashan the Cook" (*Jiashan Dienzuo*) in the company of famous Chan masters such as Jhaozhou (778–897), Yangshan (807–83), Yunmen (864–949), and Deshan (782–865) (ZZ135.800a).

41 The story referred to appears in fascicle 6 of the *Jingde Record* (*Jingde Chuandeng Lu*):

> Once when the teacher [Baizhang] was working with Guishan he asked, "Have you any fire, or not?" Guishan said, "I have." The teacher said, "Where is it?" Guishan took a stick of wood, blew on it two or three times, and passed it to the teacher. The teacher said, "It is like wood hollowed out by insects" (T51.249c28-250a1).

42 This passage alludes to case 18 of the kōan collection *Gateless Barrier* (*Wumenguan*):

> A monk asked Dongshan, "What is buddha like?" Dongshan replied, "Three pounds of hemp" (T 48.295b5-5).

An Introductory Guide to *Instructions for the Cook*

Renpō Niwa

The Place of *Instructions for the Cook* Within Dōgen's Writings

Dōgen's writings may be divided according to content into two major groups. The first group includes those texts that explore the theoretical aspects of Buddhism, such as *Shōbōgenzō*, *Eihei Kōroku*, and *Hōkyōki*. The second consists of works describing Buddhist practice, such as *Fukan Zazengi*, *Gakudō Yōjinshū*, and *Eihei Shingi*. Obviously, the doctrinally oriented writings are very important, but since Buddhism is not simply a theoretical religion Dōgen's practically oriented writings are of unique and special value. Although both Western and East Asian civilization have gained much through the ebb and flow of different currents of thought, Buddhism emphasizes not only ideas but practice. One might even say that the basic presupposition of the Buddha's teachings is that neither sensual indulgence nor thought can bring happiness. What will, then? The Buddha's answer is that we can become happy only through a combination of thought and action. Therefore, we should live according to our best understanding of life and undertake spiritual practice very diligently. I believe this is the fundamental appeal of Buddhism that has allowed it to spread around the world over the past two and one-half millennia.

Instructions for the Cook is included within the *Eihei Shingi* (*Rules of Purity for Eiheiji*). In addition to *Instructions for the Cook*, this collection includes a text called *Chiji Shingi* (*Pure Standards for Temple Administrators*). This latter text also contains instructions for the tenzo, who is one of the six temple administrators. That Dōgen wrote the separate chapter *Instructions for the Cook* in addition to this indicates how much he emphasized the position of tenzo. My own guess as to why he took the position of tenzo so seriously is that Buddhist practice is very closely related to everyday life and among the three elements of daily life—clothing, food, and housing—food is the most important.

Organization of the Text

It is convenient to divide *Instructions for the Cook* into the following five sections.

Preface This is the general introduction to the text as a whole. The main point made here is that the job of tenzo is crucial and suitable only for masters, lofty people who have awakened their hearts and minds.

The Work of Cooking Beginning with the words, "The duties of the cook over the course of a single day and night," Dōgen scrupulously describes how the tenzo should prepare and cook breakfast and lunch. First he describes how the actual work is to be done, then the attitude with which it is to be undertaken.

The Work of Serving Next, starting with his description of himself as a "mountain monk" training at Tiantong Monastery, Dōgen explains the attitude required in serving meals, along with a description of the actual way in which the work is undertaken. It is here that he offers his famous accounts of the tenzo Yong and the tenzo at Mount Ashoka Monastery, men who deeply impressed Dōgen with their dedication to the vocation of tenzo.

An Attitude That Avoids Selection and Discrimination Beginning with a quotation from the Chinese manual known as *Rules of Purity for Chan Monasteries*, Dōgen describes the overall attitude one should maintain while serving as tenzo. After describing in several ways the importance of avoiding any form of mental picking and choosing or discrimination, he provides the negative example of how the position of tenzo was abused at Kenninji, where he practiced before going to China and briefly after his return.

Joyful Mind, Nurturing Mind, and Magnanimous Mind Returning to the subject of tenzo practice in China, Dōgen reveals that the monks who held administrative positions there did so with an attitude that befitted the dharma. In his own terms, this involves the maintenance of three separate qualities, which he describes as the joyful mind, nurturing mind, and magnanimous mind.

Important Themes

The following themes included in *Instructions for the Cook* are, I believe, particularly important to its overall message.

Appointing Experienced Monks as Tenzo At the very beginning of the text, Dōgen emphasizes the profound importance of the position of tenzo. It is only "senior monks who have the way-seeking mind—eminent persons who have aroused the thought of awakening" who are to receive this assignment. Were this not the case, and a new disciple without sufficient training in zazen were given this position, the atmosphere of the monastery would become unsettled. It would also make the new disciple think that the job of tenzo is just busywork, leading him to misunderstand the buddha dharma as a whole.

Mutual Consent In the second section of *Instructions for the Cook*, Dōgen gives guidelines by which the tenzo is to consult the director and assistant director, and all monastic administrators in the course of his work. Thus the tenzo position is not restricted to work in the kitchen, but is undertaken in coordination with that of other administrators. When many people live together, they must help and support each other, so all administrative appointees must discuss their tasks and exchange opinions with each other. If one of them were so arrogant as to believe he could handle the matters of his department solely by his own judgment, and demonstrated such an attitude in his work, this would immediately become a source of disharmony within the community.

Self-Reliance Dōgen requires that the tenzo select the rice and prepare the vegetables himself, rather than delegating them to one of his assistants. These jobs are fundamental; they are the very starting-point of cooking. Of course, he cannot personally handle every detail either, as that would devolve into a tense sort of micro-management that would ruin the confidence of those working under him and disturb the orderly functioning of the kitchen and the community as a whole.

Cleanliness and Neatness When Dōgen says to put utensils that belong up high in high places and those that belong down low in low places, he is describing a situation we might say involves "a place for everything and everything in its place." The basic principle here is one of cleanliness and neat orderliness, which is a fundamental principle to be maintained in cooking, no matter whether during the ancient past or today.

Non-attachment to the Quality of Ingredients Dōgen writes that, whether dealing with the "crudest greens" or the "finest cream," when preparing food one should neither loathe nor belittle, neither rejoice in nor praise the materials one receives. Rather, one should maintain one's attitude unchanged and prepare the meal as best one can. This is a general message that pertains to all those who have entered training in Buddhism: We should cope with everything in calmness, without becoming merry or disheartened in times of success or failure. Even if the financial situation makes preparing delicious meals difficult, one must make them as delicious as possible.

Attending Morning and Evening Service Not even a single morning or evening service of ritual, scriptural recitation, and meditation may be missed on account of being appointed tenzo. The job of tenzo is important, and there is a natural tendency for a tenzo to believe it is so important that other forms of practice are irrelevant. Dōgen understood this and left a warning message for his successors, so that no such misunderstanding should occur.

Precise Awareness of Quantities Dōgen exhorts the tenzo to "close your eyes and clearly envision" the number of trainees, officers, seniors, infirmary patients, and guests currently residing in the temple, verifying any uncertainties with the appropriate officers. Then the tenzo must calculate the quantity of food necessary to feed that number, down to a single grain or a half-grain of rice. Obviously, Dōgen had a scrupulous personality, never leaving anything half done!

Being Tenzo Is the Practice of the Buddha Dharma In what are no doubt the most famous stories in *Instructions for the Cook*, Dōgen describes his personal encounters with the tenzos at Tiantong and Mount Ashoka Monasteries. His goal is to show that the job of tenzo is itself the practice of the buddha dharma. And the buddha dharma is not something that can be accomplished by proxy! The words of the old monk, "Others are not me," convey this message most eloquently. How could one leave such an important and precious task to others?

The Sincerity of Service Dōgen writes, "This is the mental attitude that the abbot has in providing for the assembly." Here he means that the most important thing the tenzo serves the assembly is the spirit of the abbot himself. More than simply providing food, each and every action of the tenzo is nothing but a manifestation of the spirit of the abbot.

Taking the Post of Tenzo Seriously Dōgen writes that when he stayed at Kenninji, just after returning from China, monks were given the position of tenzo "in name only," with no one actually carrying out the position. Perhaps this was because people then did not understand the position of tenzo and its importance, but even today we must still be careful about this.

Realization of the Way Dōgen cites the cases of Guishan and Dongshan, who furthered their practice while they were tenzos. Seven or eight hundred years have passed since Dōgen was alive, and perhaps during those years hundreds or thousands of people have attained understanding of reality while working as tenzo.

The Three Minds for All Temple Administrators Anyone who has the opportunity to engage in Buddhist practice and become ordained is indescribably fortunate. If one is offered this position which allows one to prepare pure food to offer to the Three Treasures, it is the cause for incomparable joy. Also, when one prepares food as tenzo one should have the sort of compassion with which a parent nurtures a child. Finally, rather than fussing over fancy poetry or appreciating the autumn moon, one who is appointed tenzo should work with an undistracted mind as great as the mountains and as deep as the oceans. In Dōgen's terms, these three attitudes are to have a joyful mind, a nurturing mind, and a magnanimous mind.

Conclusion

To outsiders the job of tenzo might look like ordinary routine work. However, from Dōgen's viewpoint it is the very core of Buddhist practice. There is no better way for one to practice Buddhism than to perform the job of tenzo.

Instructions for the Cook was written soon after Dōgen returned from China to Japan. Each and every sentence of this writing is filled with his burning spirit and his strong wish to spread the authentic teachings of the Buddha throughout Japan. Every time I read the text, I cannot help but be deeply moved by it.

PART II

Practice for Your Whole Life

A Monk's Mouth Is Like an Oven

Shundō Aoyama

How Shall We Burn Our Life Force?

Thirty years have passed since I was ordained as a monk. The ancient Chinese Zen master Mazu Daoyi said, "Though I have been loafing around for thirty years, I haven't ever lacked for salt and soy sauce." My own life has not been such "loafing around" in awakening. I have been loafing around in delusions and dreams, but somehow I have been allowed to walk the Way.

Thirty years ago, when I was a very new monk, I was always last in line, after all the senior monks. One day one of them asked our teacher a question and she replied, "A monk's mouth is like an oven."[1] Since I was only sixteen years old, I understood the phrase as simply saying that monks have to eat everything without expressing like and dislike. So I didn't pay particular attention to the exchange and just thought what a funny question it was. Recently, this expression popped up in my mind quite suddenly and I suddenly realized that "a monk's mouth" is not literally the mouth on my face. This "mouth" is my very life, and many different kinds of food come into it throughout my life. This mouth is the whole universe including heaven and earth.

One day not long ago, I received a phone call from a former tea-ceremony student who hadn't called me for a long time. Her voice was urgent: "Sensei! My husband has died of cancer! The memorial service is just over and I wanted to hear your voice." Not long after, I received a phone call from a childhood friend, who told me that her son, a university student, had committed suicide. These phone calls made me think about all the kinds of firewood that leap into the oven of our life, even if we want to reject them. A husband's death, a son's death, or our own death, all these logs go in. How should we burn this firewood?

An oven does not discriminate between fancy firewood and thorns. It accepts everything without preference and transforms it into thermal energy to cook rice or to heat bathwater. Pleasure and sadness, failure and success, love and hatred, all different kinds of firewood come into the oven of our lives. How can we go about accepting and burning them all, transforming them into the energy of our lives? If we complain and become sulky, our lives become smoky and we cannot burn anything. And when we become smoky, we disturb others.

A poem I found in a newspaper echoed my thoughts:[2]

A wastebasket
accepts everything.
Even the wastepaper
of my unintentional mistakes
it accepts without complaint.

A wastebasket not only accepts everything quietly, it also reclaims everything so it can all be returned to the world. This wastebasket is the same as the mouth of the universe. This is the spirit of the oven that embraces both happiness and unhappiness, loss and gain, and is one with the fundamental source that gives us life and death. This is the Buddha's life itself.

The life of a monk who takes refuge in the Buddha is also nothing other than Buddha's life itself. People's lives and each and every single thing are within the hand of Buddha, within the oven, whether we are aware of it or not. When we are enabled to awaken to that reality, the wounds we have suffered in life become the very light of Buddha and illuminate our lives, and with that, we can honor our mistakes. After loafing around as a monk for thirty years, it is only lately that I have been able to take this broad view of Dogen's phrase "a monk's mouth is like an oven."

Nurturing Mind: Putting Ourselves in Another's Place

I made a vow to work in the monastery kitchen as tenzo during *sesshin* (intensive zazen retreat) for one year as my practice of gratitude, even though I was the abbess. I worked in the kitchen from four in the morning until nine in the evening. When I saw the dishes that were brought back from the zendo after one meal using ōryōki (nested bowls used for formal meals in the zendo), I was shocked. Almost all the dishes were rinsed and wiped clean, but two plates still had vegetables on them. At practice centers it is prohibited to leave food uneaten, so I wondered what had happened. When I took a close look at these plates, I found a dead insect on the greens on each plate. Two monks in the zendo must have found the dead insects on their greens, felt bewildered about whether they should eat the bugs, and finally left the greens though they probably felt guilty about it.

Dōgen's instructions say, "First, pick over the rice. If there are any insects, green beans, hulls, or pebbles, carefully pick them out." I had washed the greens with great care, but I had missed those two insects. When I was giving a lecture after the sesshin, I apologized to the group for my careless mistake.

When I was a child, a school teacher from Shinshū (the old name for Nagano Prefecture) boarded at my temple. The teacher talked about a mistake he had made when he taught in Aichi Prefecture. In Shinshū informal tea practice is popular, and families invite guests to have steeped green tea (*sencha*) on the porch. In Aichi the formal tea ceremony (*chanoyu*) is preferred; visitors are invited to have powdered tea made ceremonially and the guest has to observe a complex ritual in drinking it.

In the bright midday heat one summer day, this teacher got thirsty and asked an old farmer he was visiting if he might have a cup of tea. The farmer, who was a tea-ceremony master, misunderstood the request and went into the house, changed his clothing, and prepared his tearoom for the formal ceremony. Since the teacher knew nothing about the formal tea ceremony, he was greatly embarrassed, but he could not escape. He awkwardly partook of a cup of tea and retreated hastily. The farmer could have ridiculed the teacher, saying, "He didn't even know how to drink a cup of tea properly!" But instead he accepted the mistake as his own, because he had misunderstood the teacher's request and unintentionally put him in an embarrassing position. After the incident the old farmer told his neighbors that the teacher was an eminent tea master, and it would be rude to give him a cup of tea in their clumsy country way. He cautioned them not to serve the teacher to protect the visitor from a repeat of that painful experience.

Sen Rikyū expressed the spirit of the tea ceremony when he said, "When you act as a host, put yourself in the place of your guest. When you are the guest, put yourself in the place of the host. A guest's mistake is the host's mistake. The host's mistake is the guest's mistake."

I returned to my mistake in the kitchen and told the group I had failed as a host because I carelessly failed to find the insects in the food.

On the other hand, the guest who returns not only the leftover food but also the plate with the insect on it shames the host. It would have been more compassionate for the monks to have wrapped the insect in a tissue and tucked it discreetly in a sleeve and to have eaten the greens even if it felt a bit unpleasant. We are not good guests if we cause pain in the tenzo's heart and put the person to shame.

Dōgen's teaching is very thorough. He says that we need to maintain the same attitude of respect toward things that we try to offer to people. We should take care of pots and bowls as well as we take care of our own eyes or head. He also says that we should consider rice and wheat as our own children. "When [the cook] watches over water and watches over grain, in every case he should sustain the caring and warmth of child-rearing." This is the attitude called nurturing mind. Instead of putting ourselves first on every occasion, we aim to cultivate a true heart toward people and things and put ourselves in the other's place at every encounter.

Magnanimous Mind: Can I Become a Shit Stick?

I am always very busy when I work as tenzo during sesshin, although we generally have only about two dozen participants, because I am such a slow worker. I can hardly even find time to go to the toilet. One day I rushed to the toilet and a thought sprang into my mind: Am I ready to become a shit stick (*kanshiketsu*)?

Such sticks used to be used like toilet paper to clean the body after bowel movements. A training monk once asked the Chinese Zen master Yunmen, "What is buddha?" Yunmen replied, "Shit stick."

Through making itself dirty, the shit stick cleans up the filth that, although it comes out of our own body, is so dirty and smells so bad that we cannot stand to be near it. If a shit stick is not a buddha, what can be? When I realized that toilet paper and shit sticks must surely be buddhas, I involuntarily bowed in *gasshō* (putting palms together). But if I were appointed to fulfill the role of shit stick, would it be possible for me to play that role with the delight and confidence I have when I am in the position of abbess? I don't think I could.

We cannot live even one day without toilet paper and we will have a mess if the garbage truck fails to come. The garbagemen are the most venerable buddhas, covered as they are with dust and excrement. I understand this in theory, and yet, if I were in such a position the deluded being within me would immediately begin to make objections.

Zen master Kōshō Uchiyama said, "A violet is a violet and a rose is a rose. Budding, blooming and withering, aging and being sick; all of these are roles we have to take. By doing our best at playing each role, we bloom as our own flower. Let's adorn the vast universe with this practice moment by moment." This is really difficult. In the world there are higher and lower roles, desirable and undesirable ones. However, when we see from the world of truth or the world of buddha, there is no waste anywhere. Everything is precious and irreplaceable, nothing is meaningless and without value.

Dōgen taught that we should do our best to play the role of tenzo or shit stick with the same attitude we would bring to playing the role of abbot. He expressed this when he admonished us, "Even when, for example, one makes a soup of the crudest greens, one should not give rise to a mind that loathes it or takes it lightly." We should neither look down on coarse greens nor be excited about preparing a fancy meal. Dōgen warned us against changing our attitude or manner of speaking depending upon what the thing is or who the person is. Such an attitude is not that of a person of the Way. Speaking about the three minds he makes the same point, saying, "Great mind is, in its spirit, like a great mountain or a great sea: it has no partiality and no factionalism." Dōgen wants to make sure we understand that whether it is the role of toilet paper or of abbot, whether it is a coarse soup or a fancy meal, we should accept these completely as one and the same buddha practice, with neither favor nor rejection, love nor hatred, and we should practice with joy and a true heart. This is what Dōgen calls magnanimous mind.

There is another story about shit sticks that shows another side of magnanimous mind: it does not ignore the differences between things. After I came back from a pilgrimage to India to the sites of Shakyamuni Buddha's life, I was talking to a doctor and I told him about the trouble I had had because I often couldn't find toilets there. The doctor told me about an experience that he had when he served in the war in Burma and Thailand as an army doctor: "Only upper class families have toilets there," he said. "Common people answer the call of nature at 'open-air toilets.' As an army doctor I was treated with respect, and sometimes people allowed me the use of their toilet. The first time I entered such an enclosure, I found something like a chopstick stand in a corner, with sticks in it. In another corner, there was another stand, but some dry stuff was caked on the sticks in it. I didn't understand what it was. Later I found out that those sticks were used as toilet paper. People washed the used sticks, dried them, and used them over and over. Japanese soldiers would come upon those sticks being dried and, thinking they were chopsticks, they would take them home as souvenirs."

The story made me laugh; even though shit sticks are necessary and important, it is a big mistake to confuse them with chopsticks. As pieces of wood, shit sticks and chopsticks are no different. We cannot call one superior and the other inferior. On the other hand, although they are one and the same wood, still chopsticks are chopsticks and shit sticks are shit sticks.

An ancient sage taught the same thing in the beautiful expression, "The colors of spring do not discriminate between high and low, but flowering branches are naturally long and short." Spring comes to all beings equally, it does not discriminate between things it likes and things it does not like. Spring neither comes earlier to things it likes nor comes later to things it doesn't like. Bathed by the equable light of spring, a violet is a violet and a rose is a rose. One branch is long, another is short. Each and every branch blooms in its own way; that is its role.

Dōgen alludes to both sides of magnanimous mind when he quotes the famous conversation between Yangshan and Guishan. Dōgen points to the universal purity of all things when he tells us to wash them so that they are completely pure and clean and he addresses the differences between things when he says to place up high those that belong in high places, and to put down low those that belong in low places. He cautions us to put each thing away in its proper place, the place where each is best settled. We should do so not carelessly or abruptly but with our true caring heart, knowing that everything is interconnected with everything else in the universe and therefore is of equal value.

Joyful Mind: Each and Every Thing Is Wonderful

A company president once told me the following story: "We were having a problem with graffiti in one of our company washrooms. Someone was scribbling repeatedly in the toilet stalls. No matter how many times we put up warning signs and painted over the scribbling, the graffiti would appear again. One day, a different message was posted, a sign board on which was written, 'Please don't make this toilet dirty with scribbling. This is my precious place of work!' It was written by an old cleaning woman in a faltering handwriting. Everyone was deeply moved by the notice and from that day on, the scribbling ceased completely." The repeated warnings failed to stop the graffiti, but it was completely halted by one sign in shaky handwriting.

Cleaning a toilet is usually looked down on, and even the janitor often feels that it is a humiliating job. And yet, this old woman declared with conviction that the toilets were her precious place of work and that her work was a valuable job. Everyone at the company admired the old woman's attitude; even the habitual offender doing the scribbling must have felt ashamed. She put her entire life energy into her job, working with nobility. Her attitude is nothing other than joyful mind.

All work without exception is wonderful work. Depending upon one's attitude, it becomes irreplaceable, wonderful work or meaningless work. When we can face any and all work with the attitude of that janitor, the encounter with work becomes complete and our lives become joyful and worth living.

I once toured an electronics factory after giving a lecture there. I was astonished to see how the workers used microscopes to assemble the extremely tiny parts. If one of those miniscule parts is assembled inaccurately, the entire mechanism fails. I saw how each and every tiny part works in the world shouldering the work of the entire watch. I thought that there is nothing so small that it is worthless or meaningless.

I realized that each household, country, and, further, this entire universe including heaven and earth exist in the same way that a watch does. From the viewpoint of ordinary human beings, there seem to be distinctions between superior and inferior, valuable and valueless; however, from the Buddha's point of view, all things are completely one without any value discrimination. The entire household, society, or universe is completely contained within each and every one of its parts. You can work with a jaundiced eye, considering yourself a worthless part of a machine, or you can do the same work with the awakened attitude that whatever your work may be, you are shouldering the entire universe, past, present, and future. There is a huge difference in the experience of life depending upon which one of these two attitudes one adopts.

When Shakyamuni Buddha was born, he pointed to heaven and earth and said, "Above and under heaven, I alone am worthy of respect." This does not mean that Buddha said he was the only great person, or the only person worthy of worship. Rather this means that each person and kind of work, every flower and bird are animated by the life that penetrates the whole of heaven and earth. Whether people awaken to that reality or not, they are shouldering this universal life as they move their hands and feet and smile or cry.

I particularly like the verse by Zen Master Xuedou that Dōgen quotes.

> One letter, seven letters, three letters, and five;
> Investigating myriads of images, one reaches no basis.
> In the depth of night, the moon sets into the dark sea;
> Seeking the black dragon's pearl, one finds there are many.

Our lives are uneven, rough, and very unpredictable, a jumble like one, seven, three, and five characters. All sorts of unexpected things happen one after another. We ordinary human beings go looking for truth and the meaning of life and so we wander here and there. However, just as the vast light of the moon is reflected on each wave, everything we encounter in our lives is important and wonderful. There is nothing worthless.

This verse expresses precisely the same point as the tenzo's answer to the young Dōgen, "One, two, three, four, five, in the whole world, it can never be hidden." To make this clear Dōgen wrote the *Instructions for the Cook*, and the other texts in *Rules of Purity for Eiheiji* like the *Dharma for Taking Food*, and the fascicles of the *Shōbōgenzō* on daily activities like "Cleaning the Body" and "Washing the Face."

Enjoy Each Step: The Four Seasons Cooperate in a Single Scene

A group of my old tea students visited me to enjoy the summer in Shinshū. We took the most essential tea utensils and went to the beach on the Azusa River, where we enjoyed a tea ceremony in the open air. After that we decided to walk to Myōjin Pond.

It was a cool, sunny day, and the green of the trees and grass was fresh; through tamaracks and white birches we could see the river, the summer light dancing on each wave. The water was so clear we could see each stone at the bottom and the water plants swaying in the current. The blue August sky was transparent and white clouds drifted by, softening the steep slope of Mount Hodaka before us. I forgot about Myōjin Pond and just enjoyed the scenery that changed with each step. We shouted happily as we searched for wild flowers and chased after dragonflies.

Then one of our group asked, "How long does it take to walk to Myōjin Pond?" Someone else said, "It is very far away. I am tired out." And another asked a group going the other way how far it was to the pond. It reminded me of a passage from Hermann Hesse, in which he wrote, as I recall it, "The eye that only seeks after the destination cannot taste the sweetness of wandering. Forests, streams, all grand sights on our way are closed to us."

Hesse said that the secret method of traveling is to taste the process of the trip. If we seek only to reach our goal hurriedly, we will lose sight of forests, streams, and the momentary brightness of starlight. Our lives are just like that. We should enjoy each step, living with the attitude that each and every step is like already being at our destination. We do need to have an end of our journey, our personal Myōjin Pond, as the direction toward which we are moving, and yet the concrete goal should be each step at that moment. We cannot predict when something may happen that will prevent us from reaching our goal. If we walk the path only for the sake of reaching our goal, then the effort of our lives will be easily thwarted and we may feel our whole life has been wasted. If we walk each and every step as the goal and appreciate the whole process as "Myōjin Pond," never to be experienced the same way again, then even if we need to put an end to our journey, we can accept it without complaining.

In the journey of our lives, what does it mean to enjoy the process? We are sometimes unsuccessful in what we do, though we work in all seriousness; people don't understand us and we feel that we have the whole world against us. At other times we are so happy we feel as if we were running through the heavens on a rainbow-colored bridge. We may some day feel as if we were at a precipitous cliff, losing a beloved husband or child, or even lacking enough food for the day. We may have to tumble down the slope of fatal sickness. Travel is more interesting if we have a variety of views, and the journeys of our lives are more enjoyable when we have multifarious scenery. All the same, we should not be overwhelmed by all that life scenery. We should just view it as the scenery of our journey and actively enjoy and appreciate it.

Dōgen said that magnanimous mind is like the great mountains or the ocean; it is not biased:

> Being drawn by the voices of spring, it does not wander into the swamp of spring. Although it sees the colors of autumn, it has nothing whatsoever of the spirit of autumn. It contrasts the four seasons against the backdrop of a single vista. It views pennyweights and ounces [of silver] within the context of a single system of measurement.

The voices of spring are the favorable circumstances in our lives and the fall colors are adverse circumstances. We are ordinary human beings who get rattled and disheartened when we meet with difficult situations, and we try to escape. When conditions are favorable, we become puffed up and lose our heads. Instead of that, we should view the vistas of the four seasons equally. We should accept happiness and unhappiness as the same kind of scenery, taste them and not be overwhelmed. Then the great nature and the actual voyage of our life unfold without being controlled by our small human desires.

We need to fling away the looking glass that reflects an egocentric view and entrust our whole body and mind to the greatness of nature. Then we will smell the perfume of plum blossoms blooming bravely in the cold wind and we will hear the quiet palpitation of spring under muddy water and the delightful sounds of grass and trees swaying in a thunderstorm.

■ ■ ■

1   This is a saying attributed to Katyayana, one of Shakyamuni Buddha's ten close disciples.
2   The poem is by Mr. Enomoto Eiichi.

Spreading the Dharma, Engaging Your Life

Dainin Katagiri

I am a practitioner who follows the teachings of Zen Master Dōgen, which I believe to be the very essence of the buddha dharma, but I want to present the following from my perspective as a missionary.[1] In teaching the dharma, the quest for enlightenment and the teaching of living beings must be identical. This is the nature of the buddha dharma, but in considering my own efforts I cannot help recognizing how far I am from this ideal. I labor at instructing others, but if I were to ignore my own aspirations to enlightenment the very mission of teaching would be undermined. The challenge is to work most effectively and seek enlightenment within the context of these activities, aware of how this very difficulty helps us to achieve our goal.

The beginning point of Buddhism is the study of human beings. From there it goes on to transcend the individualities of human life, and then returns home again to human beings. Buddhism should therefore be understandable by everyone, regardless of culture or ethnic background. Even if we wear the costumes of different ages, nations, cultures, and manners of thinking, once we throw away these costumes we return to one and the same state of humanity, which in Buddhism we refer to as buddha nature. Only thus can the essence of Buddhism be understood, and then it will be transmitted as easily as water entering loose, dry soil. The differences of individual humans and their cultures will necessarily lead to variations in how Buddhism is understood and how it may be applied to everyday life. Without a profound understanding of a particular society it is difficult to engage in successful missionary activity in that society, so in order to present Dōgen's teaching on spiritual self-cultivation, I have had to investigate the cultural realm in which I live and work.

America is characterized by an unusual degree of tolerance. Diverse faiths and value systems, changing moral and sexual codes, radical fashions and traditional cultures—whatever one might point to, not only are there Americans doing it, but there are other Americans trying to accept it.

Most of the world has come to value the individual and freedom of choice, and Americans in particular act on their opportunities to travel, to study, to live in foreign cultures, and to turn away from their own traditional culture. But the more people value the freedom to choose, the more they find commensurate problems coming up in their lives. The very freedom to choose seems to lead to uncertainty, and to the suffering of anxiety, fear, and loneliness.

The United States has a huge expanse of land, a variety of races from all over the world, and the many cultures that those people have brought with them. In spite of this heterogeneity, and perhaps because of it, too, the overall society maintains a miraculous equilibrium. The United States can be seen as the world's most advanced country in terms of culture, the degree of human suffering, and the treatment of human suffering. I feel that because of this combination very few countries have better conditions for establishing the Buddhist sangha.

Engaging the Way

The natural sciences deal with things objectively, as they are, and attempt to discover their realities. But through the natural sciences we cannot find the subject, that "thing in itself" that interacts with the phenomenal world. Dissatisfaction with this limitation has led to tremendous fruit in the social sciences, such as philosophy, psychology, and ethics. Nevertheless, this is not enough. After all, these disciplines are merely objective studies of the subject. Ultimately we have to depend on Buddhism, especially on the teaching of Dōgen, to understand the subject, and to apprehend how to deal with it.

To fulfill our humanity, we must not ignore the objects we encounter. One great human virtue is our ability to live creatively with objects, but if our intelligence functions only for the sake of humans, then it is like a wild boar rushing about, ignoring things and kicking them away. When intelligence is used so that both humans as subject and things as object coexist peacefully here and now, this is the way for humans to live humanely. In Dōgen's terms, this is called "engaging the way" (bendō).

There is no fixed form for engaging the way. It is about how to live intimately with things. However, this "how to" is not a question. Questions require our discriminating mind, but this "how to" means that we are in the process of living, for which there is no fixed form. We are just in the process of living in the best way here and now, together with all things, with the true mind, the sincere mind, and purity. When we try to explain this and ask questions about it, only "how?" remains. And this interrogative itself is nothing but the vibrant activity of invigorated life.

Dōgen recalled being instructed about words and engaging the way by the tenzo at Mount Ashoka Monastery. "Words" means all beings in the phenomenal world. Generally speaking, all the phenomena we comprehend have been at some point filtered through our consciousness. They are already conceptualized. If they are not conceptualized, they are not understandable. The phenomenal world is like a massive cryptogram. Even without being decoded, every element in the cryptogram can communicate with every other one, and all the elements thus become mutually intimate with each other and thereby really exist. It is a very peaceful panoramic world. In that world, the harmony of all beings is maintained with perfect purity and without any discrimination. This is the aspect of reality called "in the whole world nothing is hidden."

For people to live truly as humans, we must live so that we can communicate intimately with each other in this state of "in the whole world nothing is hidden." We must manifest this in our every action here and now, instead of just explaining it. In this effort there are no fixed forms such as, "if you act this way things will turn out this way," or "if you act that way things will lead that way." There is no way other than to keep watching the world of ever-changing objects with eyes wide open and to maintain the attitude of "how to live." This is engaging the way. If we are not tuned to "in the whole world nothing is hidden," our practice cannot be called engaging the way.

Diligently Carry on the Way

Dōgen wrote, "During the day and through the night, whether things come and dwell in your mind or your mind turns and dwells on things, put yourself on a par with them and diligently engage the way."

The view "in the whole world nothing is hidden" to which we must attune ourselves never exists outside of human life. When we treat everything we encounter with true mind, sincere mind, and purity, those things respond to us with true mind, sincere mind, and purity. Human beings and things are born together, and we practice together. Human life is conveyed to things, and the things to which human life is conveyed support our human life. The life thus supported and continued is not limited just to human beings. It permeates all things, so that they all communicate subtly with each other. There is no ownership of this life, so it is called the Buddha's life. If we can deeply accept this in our hearts, we cannot help but continue living with the attitude of "things come to mind and the mind attends to them." Dōgen said that this is to be at one with them all, while diligently undertaking the way. You must make it an ongoing undertaking of the way, aiming to live and practice at one with things "all day and all night," not only in certain situations but in every situation, whether favorable or adverse, sleeping or waking.

To love the mountains is not to know about mountains, but to climb mountains and to live and die continuously with them. Then the mountains themselves speak to us frankly about the infinite world of the mountains, which human beings otherwise never know.

Burning Your Life

Mount Fuji is a symbol of beauty in Japanese culture. As depicted in art works and seen through the windows of the bullet train, it really is very beautiful. But this is just a part of the beauty of Mount Fuji. The best way to realize the true beauty of Mount Fuji is to actually go climb it. If you do that, the beauty of Mount Fuji as you have known it will disappear. What you will experience will be just the intense effort it takes to climb the mountain and the pain caused by that effort. But this does not mean that the true beauty of Mount Fuji has disappeared. The beauty of Mount Fuji is eternal and unchanging, however human beings may critique or appraise it.

Within the activity of climbing we can eventually come to feel the meaning of life. This cannot be defined as the beauty of Mount Fuji, or as anything else in particular. When we live with Mount Fuji and breathe with Mount Fuji, we can experience the deep taste of being at one with Mount Fuji. We are already beyond the realm of "trying to understand."

An individual must take the initiative to live and practice with things. This is engaging the way. Engaging the way is not someone else's business. If you yourself do not practice on all occasions, you are not really undertaking engaging the way no matter how well you may be able to explain it.

The importance of engaging the way in every single moment is readily apparent in Dōgen's *Instructions for the Cook*. When Dōgen sympathized with the labors of an aged tenzo and suggested others could do his work, the tenzo answered, "Others are not me." It was not somebody else's work, but his work. When Dōgen suggested he could do it another day, the tenzo said, "What time should I wait for?" In other words, the way is to be cultivated at all times, in every moment. This was a powerful statement, forcefully conveying what engaging the way is all about to Dōgen. He recalled, "I immediately withdrew. Thinking to myself as I walked away, I deeply appreciated that his job expresses the essential function." Behind the words "I immediately withdrew" we can feel how shocked Dōgen was, we can hear the cry of pain that shock caused him, as if a sharp knife had been plunged deep into his chest. This cry gradually became the calm reflection described by the simple words, "I deeply appreciated that his job expresses the essential function."

Engaging the way is "what time should I wait for?"; it is "others are not me." It is to continuously burn your life in the position of tenzo and in everything you do.

Dōgen describes three attitudes necessary to fulfill administrative roles within Song-dynasty Chinese monasteries: practice so as to perfectly and completely benefit both self and others, make the sangha thrive and revitalize its standards, and work hard to stand shoulder to shoulder with our predecessors.

When we perform *gasshō*, placing the palms together, we continuously burn our lives in the activity of gasshō itself. At this time, gasshō settles down in gasshō and the self settles down in the self. To continuously burn one's life in each thing one encounters is not just to do things without considering the risk to one's own life. Our actions must be undertaken to benefit others and to make things alive as they are. When we eat daikon pickles, chewing quietly without making noise, we are making daikon pickles alive, and we are also engaging in the single color of diligently practicing the way together with others. It must never be a self-centered practice, but always one focused on benefiting others. Practicing to benefit others is simultaneously the pure activity of continuously burning one's life in the world of encountering daikon pickles. What is unfolding here is the world in which everything is communicating intimately with everything else.

This practice of perfectly and fully benefiting both self and others also becomes the foundation on which we help the sangha thrive and renew its standards. The third point, to work shoulder to shoulder with those who have come before us, is the most important attitude, especially in modern times. If we ignore the examples of our predecessors for the reason that America is different, or we are ordinary, that is like making red beans and rice without red beans. Even if we keep practicing that way for hundreds or thousands of eons, we will never hit the mark.

Let us consider the following words of Dōgen:

> The way to put that aspiration into practice in one's own person is, for example, to take the same three coins that one's predecessors spent to make a soup of the crudest greens and use them now to make a soup of the finest cream. This is difficult to do. Why is that? Because present and past are completely different, like the distance between heaven and earth. How could we ever be able to equal their stature? Nevertheless, when we work attentively, therein lies the principle that makes it possible to surpass our predecessors.

Dōgen is not urging us to be more clever than the ancients. He is not saying that we can spend our three coins more effectively than they did, or that we can make better food than they did by having a better attitude. Differences of era and culture make it difficult to follow the way of the ancients, but if we do not follow them, we are just doing things in our own style, and it is nothing but entertaining ourselves like kittens chasing their own tails. If we can make the wild horses and monkeys in the forest of our minds take the backward step of inner illumination, then even in the moment of our encounter with a single vegetable stalk, naturally the world of becoming completely one, in which self and vegetable become one, will unfold. And then, by truly following our predecessors, we surpass them.

"Without stirring a single atom or disturbing a single form" we enter into "mystical cooperation with all dharmas, and completely penetrate all times."[2] It becomes the wonderful performance of a great symphony. This is the way of burning one's life continuously and completely, to the limit, in each thing and event that one encounters. This is called "buddha's work." Here only the world of benefiting others exists. It is the reality of the most humble, quiet, and vivid practice of the path, without any arrogance whatsoever.

Zen Buddhism in America is still an infant from the viewpoint of Dōgen's teaching. But in the limited environment given to me I have tried to use all possible means to bring Dōgen's teaching closer to people who are seriously seeking the path. At the very least I always try to teach and practice the basic attitude of practice that I have described here with reference to *Instructions for the Cook*. I will keep walking this same way as long as I am allowed to.

■ ■ ■

1   Dainin Katagiri trained at Eiheiji and came to the United States in 1963, first to the Zenshuji Sōtō Zen Mission in Los Angeles and then to Sōkōji and the San Francisco Zen Center, both in San Francisco. In 1972 he moved to Minnesota, where he founded the Minnesota Zen Meditation Center.
2   This passage is from Dōgen's *Bendōwa*.

Mendicant Practice in Buddha's World

Zengan Hashimoto

Learning about Religious Begging

When I was a young monk and newly arrived at my training monastery, I went on my first begging rounds (*takuhatsu*) with five senior monks. We got up at one o'clock in the morning to begin walking to a town fifteen miles away. I had never done mendicant practice before, so I was not sure I could chant without hesitation the phrase I was supposed to say, "Please donate a small token of your generosity for the temple." But when we reached a village on our way and I began to chant, I realized to my surprise that my state of mind was the same as during one of the walking chants in the dharma hall.

At the monastery, the young monks in training complained of the perpetual sutra chanting that began early in the morning and took the place of scheduled lecture times almost every day, and for which evening zazen was often canceled. On that begging expedition I first realized that chanting sutras while walking was a precious practice.

One day when I was begging in a town near the monastery, I stopped in front of a farmer's house and noticed that all the family members were working on the roof replacing the thatch. I had come at a bad time, and was about to leave when I saw the wife climbing down from the roof. She opened a rice storage box. Finding no rice in it, she opened another box, but it seemed there was no rice in this box either. I could not just go while she continued to look around for rice, so I stood there, wondering what to do. Suddenly she picked up a lunchbox and scooped up some rice from a pan on the stove. She gave me the rice and sent me off bowing toward me with her hands together in *gasshō*. I walked away feeling her gasshō at my back, and I silently pledged to pursue zazen practice even more intently. I recognized that there was no excuse for not pursuing the buddha dharma with sincerity since I was receiving food that could fill families' stomachs. I made up my mind to sit all night without lying down from that night on. Since I was by nature a lazy person, it was not easy for me to keep this pledge for long, but I will never forget the incident.

The Buddha said, "When a monk receives food while begging, he should eat it with the intensity of a child eating during a famine." Some people speak ill of ritual begging, commenting that monks who live by mendicancy for even three days cannot bear to give up this lifestyle. They do not understand that mendicancy is a serious discipline, far different from the activity of a street beggar.

One day I stood in front of a farmer's house in a corner of a town. I chanted for a while, but no one appeared. Since I had a feeling that I would get a donation, I kept standing there. Suddenly a small child came from behind me and gave me some coins. The child did not seem to come out of the house, so I continued to stand in front of it. Soon a woman came out of the house with a bowl of rice. I was still wondering whose child had given me the money and turned around to find his house. I saw a young woman in the shadow of a small house across the field, bowing to me. I had not planned to visit her home since I thought it was just a storage hut. The young mother had asked her child to bring me the money because she did not expect a monk to come to her house, as it was so humble.

At the back entrance of the monks' hall in my monastery, there was a signboard listing regulations that were read aloud in the evening before a practice period (*ango*) began.[1] One of the regulations for monks was that while out begging a monk should never pass by even a small house. When I saw the young woman bowing to me, I finally began to understand the power of the Buddha's rule.

Saving Self and Others Together

The practice of ritual begging is not only for supporting monks' lives. When people want to give, their generosity comes from the boundless buddha mind and makes the boundary between self and others drop away. The purpose of mendicancy is to give everyone the opportunity to open the gate to Buddha's pure land.

It was very common to receive no response in commercial areas with many big shops, but in poor neighborhoods, people would flock from all over, fighting to bring me a little of their hard-earned savings. They made me their buddha.

One winter day we set out on begging rounds, but it was snowing hard. The snow was piled up to our waists and every monk hoped that the event would be called off. Once they realized that there was no hope of that, they went out into the snow with little hope of receiving offerings.

The people who were living in the area had no prior experience with such heavy snow, so nobody knew how to plow and open a path. We struggled to walk through the snow and by the time I reached the first house, I was soaked. A man leapt out of the house where I began to chant. He offered to let me stay a while to dry my robes and made a fire in the fireplace. Then he called the children who were sitting around the heater (*kotatsu*) and introduced me. Everyone came out and saw me off with gasshō when I left. After that, I could not skip any of the other houses in the area. Having received such warm care, I saw how in mendicancy we benefit others as well as ourselves.

There was one family that never donated to any monks. They lived in a mansion and seemed rich, although there were rumors that they had fallen on hard times. Monks challenged the family to open up their minds and accept us, but no one succeeded in exchanging conversation with them, even when the woman of the house was working directly in front of the monks. I believe our efforts were not good enough to touch their hearts.

There is a story about a household like that in India a long time ago. Every day a virtuous monk visited the house on his begging rounds. For seven years, the rich man did not give anything to the monk. After seven years, one day the man of the house went out and only his wife was there when the monk arrived. Unexpectedly, the wife spoke to the monk, saying, "Please skip my house." Upon hearing even these few words, the monk was so happy he left the house with a smile. At the gate, the monk met the rich man just coming home. Seeing the monk's smile, the rich man thought his wife had given something to the monk. He asked the monk, who answered with a big smile, "Yes, she certainly did."

The rich man was furious to hear this and accused his wife of having given something to the monk, but she denied it. The rich man was very upset that the monk had lied to him. The next day he waited for the monk so he could accuse him of lying.

As expected, the monk came to the house to ask for a donation. The rich man denounced him, saying, "You are a Buddhist monk. Buddhist monks should not lie. My wife did not give you anything yesterday, but you told me you got a donation from her." The monk said to the rich man, "I have come to your house every day for seven years, but I have never received anything. Nobody gave me so much as a word until yesterday, when your wife merely said, 'Please skip my house.' I was so pleased to have her talk to me. That is what I received from her."

The rich man had thought that the monk only wanted tangible goods, but the monk received all gifts happily, even intangible words. After this the rich man became a great supporter of the monk, and his son became the monk's disciple. The name of the monk was Siggava and the son was named Moggaliputta Tissa. The son served as the chairman of the third council of the Buddha's disciples under the patronage of King Ashoka, wrote *Ronji Issensō* (*One Thousand Chapters on Topics of Dharma Discussion*) and devoted his life to spreading the dharma. Great Siggava's seven years of mendicant practice thus contributed to the making of a great Buddhist leader.

Mendicancy is a hard form of training that aims not only to help the monastery but also to help monks become free from their selfishness. Simultaneously, in our mendicant practice, buddhas manifest and express the dharma and enable people to awaken to buddha mind, the spirit of compassion for others. In any situation, we should maintain our faith that all beings are buddha nature. Without abandoning anyone, we should continue patiently to lead people into the world of buddha.

When I was in the army briefly, I had a chance to take the other role. I was paid little money, but when I met poor people I could not stop myself from giving them what I had. For me, each person was a reflection of myself. No matter what I gave them, whether money or help, I felt that these deeds were for my own salvation as much as for theirs. The act of making offerings has the power to save the self and other simultaneously.

The Tradition of Mendicancy

As Ananda was setting out on begging rounds, the Buddha said to him, "Now you have a mendicant's bowl, thus you have to live following the rules of the seven buddhas of the past." Mendicant practice has been handed down from the far-off time of the seven buddhas of the past, and as long as the buddha way is practiced, mendicancy should be maintained. Selflessness is the basis of buddha dharma, and the faithful practice of mendicancy is important for studying, expressing, and practicing selflessness.

Buddhist monks are not allowed to save things for the future but have to live by the goodwill of the people, tied to them by mutual trust. The monk must not be lazy and behave in a manner that will lead to distrust. He should resolve to starve to death if he fails to receive support from people; a monk who worries about his health and survival is not a true disciple of the Buddha. Even now when our lives are so different, we should maintain this spirit of mendicant practice.

The mendicant should not try to force a donor to give against his will, but should be patient, like the Buddha, who accepted offerings but did not ask for them. His monks received their meals from the people's will, sharing what they received with their whole community. This spirit lives on in the meal ceremony in contemporary monasteries. Before starting to eat, monks hold up their bowl and chant, "I will share the meal equally with first, the three treasures, Buddha, Dharma, and Sangha; second, the four benefactors, our parents, teachers, leaders, and the world; and third, the six realms of samsara, hell beings, hungry ghosts, animals, fighting spirits, human beings, and heavenly beings."

In the early years of the Buddha's era, cooking was not allowed where Buddhist monks stayed for a while to practice, but gradually settled monasteries developed and a place to cook was needed. This was the origin of the tenzo's department, although cooking areas were then built outside the boundary of the monastery compound, separate from the monks' quarters.

Later in India and again when Buddhism was introduced to China, the rules of the Buddha's era were transformed. The aristocracy, high-ranking officials, and the rich patronized the sangha. Appreciation for mendicant practice was reduced and monks merely walked through the streets to receive donations. Isolated from ordinary society, monks stayed in their monasteries, supporting their lives by being obsequious to the rich.

Criticizing this lifestyle that was corrupting Buddhism, some monks left this comfortable life for the mountains, where they cultivated the land for food, built huts to undertake the way through the practice of zazen, and created a new approach to Buddhist practice. They purposely violated Buddhist regulations that did not allow monks to cut grass and trees or to cultivate land. A new era had begun, of monks living by the motto, "A day of no work is a day of no eating." The rules of purity (*shingi*) for training in Zen temples were established on this basis.

As the number of these monks grew, the sangha could not support the monks just by their own labor. Zen monasteries began to own manors and to receive donations from supporters, at which point large cooking facilities were required. The cooking facilities became an important place for practice. Probably this was begun by the time the first Zen monastic regulations were compiled, these attributed to Zen master Baizhang Huaihai.

Dōgen wrote *Instructions for the Cook* to promote Baizhang's idea, calling kitchen work single-flavor Zen or the single-color practice. The work of the tenzo seems far different from living by mendicancy, but they are animated by the same selfless ideals, and both are practices of Buddha's children for carrying out Buddha's work.

For the Tenzo, Rolling Up the Sleeves Is the Mind of the Way

Patience and hard work are the most important virtues for the tenzo, just as they are for the mendicant monk. Every day the tenzo has to prepare three meals. He washes the rice, cooks, takes care of the pots as carefully as if they were his own body and uses water as if it were his life. Only a serious worker can do this. In this regard the tenzo's duty and mendicant practice are identical.

The stories of two diligent tenzos are central to *Instructions for the Cook*. One was the tenzo of Mount Ashoka Monastery, who set out after lunch on a twelve-mile trip to the ship Dōgen was on, to purchase mushrooms for the next day's special meal. The monk refused Dōgen's invitation to a meal and returned to the monastery to prepare for the next day. The old monk devoted himself to serving delicious meals to other monks and did not question the hard work despite his age.

The other was the old tenzo drying mushrooms on a mat under the hot sun at Tiantong Monastery. He was covered in sweat, yet he pushed himself to finish the work because, as he said, "Other people are not me."

It is not only tenzos who need such a work ethic; no one can practice the buddha way without such a diligent attitude. As far as I know, everyone who has attained the way has maintained this spirit, abandoning selfishness and covetousness.

Buddha's virtue was manifested by his shortening his life from its full span of a hundred years and dying when he was eighty years old. It is said that he did this in order to donate the offerings he would have received during the succeeding twenty years to his followers in later generations. Today monks can live by donations from people because we inherit the blessings of Buddha's donation of twenty years of his life. When we accept donations, we have to remember that they have not been offered because of our own virtue. They are given to the Buddha, and we receive them in place of the Buddha.

In *Instructions for the Cook* Dōgen urges us not to discuss the quality and quantity of donated foods. When the tenzo respects the offering regardless of the quality, the donor will be happy, the monks will be happy, and the donations will be fully utilized. These harmonious relations create the world of buddha in which donor, receiver, and offering are all empty and free from clinging. Therefore, to cook rice and to make soup in the kitchen are as valuable as practicing in the monks' hall. Cooking rice and making side dishes become the kōan, "What is Buddha?" "Three pounds of hemp." Our practice is not different from acts as ordinary as drinking tea and cooking rice.

Food in a monastery is provided by faithful donors; it results from the Buddha's generosity. There is no place in this for evaluation of flavor or quality. It is nonsense to say that if monks eat delicious meals then it is easy to become a buddha or that if monks eat distasteful foods, then they will become hungry ghosts. If a donor gives food with true faith and the tenzo serves that meal with a full heart, the meal is tasty even if it is only half a bowl of rice gruel.

I recall monks who worked hard and with a great deal of spirit when we did not have enough to eat, while some tended to work and practice with less enthusiasm when there was a lot of fancy food. From the viewpoint of nurturing the sacred body to attain the way, there is no distinction between fancy and ordinary foods.

Dōgen introduced a precious mealtime ceremony to Japan. When the preparations for a meal are done, it is placed on the kitchen altar and the tenzo offers incense and does nine prostrations facing the monks' hall. The tenzo prostrates three times each for the three treasures of buddha, dharma, and sangha. The tenzo performs this ceremony, but it is done on behalf of the donors, the cooks, and whoever had any contact with preparing the meal.

During begging rounds, people making donations often send us off with gasshō, and some want to give monks even the last scoop of rice from their storage box because they see the monks practice wholeheartedly for the sake of the dharma despite their poverty and hard training. Reflecting on the bodhi mind that inspires monks to practice for the sake of truth, donors arouse the same bodhi mind and give food to the monks as their own devotion to Buddhism. The donors' contributions encourage the monks to work and practice harder to pursue the buddha dharma. The mutual respect between monks and donors caused by this bodhi mind is what makes mendicancy possible. Using the donated foods, the tenzo cooks for the monks who serve the three treasures. The tenzo is not the donor, but only prepares the food offering. But the tenzo's diligence, patience, and single-mindedness are themselves a pure offering. The tenzo's nine prostrations at the final stage of preparation of a meal expresses this mind of gasshō, of selfless giving, on behalf of all the meal's donors.

The Significance of Words and Practice

When Dōgen was young, he thought that Zen should only be practiced by doing zazen or by seeking the meaning of kōans. When he arrived in China, waiting for permission to leave the ship, he was stunned by his encounter with the tenzo of Mount Ashoka Monastery, who had come to the ship to buy mushrooms. At the end of the encounter the tenzo said to him with loud laughter, "You, who came from a foreign land, do not know the true meaning of Buddhist practice. You also do not understand the true meaning of words." In his astonishment, Dōgen experienced a new perspective on Zen Buddhism.

When Dōgen met the same tenzo later, at Tiantong Monastery, he asked him further about the true meaning of words and of wholehearted practice. The tenzo answered, "Words are one, two, three, four, and five, and the true practice of Buddhism is 'nothing is ever hidden.'" True practice is to recognize this world as it is. "One, two, three, four, and five" means that one must do things one by one. As a tenzo, one must clean the rice, cook the rice and vegetables, and mindfully put things away in suitable places. Everything a tenzo does is done in order, like one, two, three, four, and five. The essence expressed in the sayings of ancient Zen masters is nothing other than each and every action in daily monastic life.

The Chinese tenzo straightforwardly expressed that "nothing is hidden within the whole world." This means that buddha dharma is completely manifested within this world. The true practice of buddha dharma lies in the truth that this world is buddha's world. The world of buddha is not something special, attainable only through zazen. Zazen is the entire world. Outside of zazen there is no special realm of enlightenment (satori) to search for. There is no hidden, mysterious buddha dharma outside of zazen.

Each step in mendicant practice is a step on buddha's land. Each house we visit is a place to meet with buddha. When we see this truth from the viewpoint of individuality, it is expressed as "one, two, three, four, and five." The same truth is expressed from the entirety of buddha mind as "never hidden in the whole world." As a tenzo, we meet with buddhas through hard work in the kitchen. We bow to the numberless buddhas throughout the whole world at each step on the street while begging. This is the true meaning of words and practice.

Being tenzo sometimes seems like an unfavorable assignment, but a tenzo can generate the wisdom of how to turn work into zazen practice, as well as having opportunities to practice hidden virtue and to help other monks through providing meals and contributing to the flourishing community practice. Through working as tenzo and giving benefit to others, we find our own practice develops.

In the case of begging, it may seem as though donors are losing their possessions through offering, but in giving, the donor's heart transcends the boundary between self and others and the donor becomes the richest person in the world. Humans are always fighting over small things, but within the heart of giving and serving, there is real richness and salvation. This is what both the *Instructions for the Cook* and mendicancy ultimately teach.

■ ■ ■

1   Monastic practice periods are ninety-day training periods of concentrated practice without leaving the monastic enclosure (except for monks going out for necessary temple business). They date back to the summer rainy-season retreats of Shakyamuni's time in India. In Japan they have traditionally been held twice a year, in summer and winter.

Kitchen Kōans

Kōryō Shinno

Kitchen work is sometimes considered a lowly, menial job that no one wants to do. At a Zen monastery, however, the position of tenzo is highly valued. The tenzo maintains the practitioners' precious lives and health. The quality of the temple's tenzo determines whether the entire group of practitioners can practice in a wholesome condition or not. In addition, it affects the economic management of the temple.

These principles apply to families as well. Anyone who takes the responsibility of cooking for a household is the same as a tenzo, taking care of all the family members' precious lives and health. A family cook's efforts help determine the family's prosperity or decline, so he or she needs to pay careful attention to the preparation of food and to the way it is eaten.

Why is kitchen work precious and important? How can we accept kitchen work as the practice of the buddha way and also as a way of developing and perfecting our character, despite its usually being considered lowly, menial work?

Dōgen points the way for tenzos, and indeed for all cooks, saying that tenzos must first arouse the spirit that "cooks regard tying up their sleeves [for manual work] as the way-seeking mind." The tenzo must also develop joyful mind, nurturing mind, and magnanimous mind. Acting diligently with these fundamental attitudes, one can create food that helps make practitioners in the community happy.

Since ancient times, masters with way-seeking mind and those who had awakened their hearts have been appointed as tenzo. Many of these masters clarified the one great matter of life and death while they were tenzo. A number of these masters' stories are recounted in *Instructions for the Cook* and in other classic Zen texts, and can tell us a great deal about the attitudes necessary for an effective tenzo or household cook.

Creating a Six-Foot-Tall Body with a Stalk of Vegetable

"Lifting a single piece of vegetable, make [yourself into] a six-foot body [i.e., a buddha] and ask that six-foot body to prepare a single piece of vegetable."

How can we accomplish this? To treat a vegetable stalk as the body of buddha, we must put our whole body and mind into whatever we are doing. Creatively cooking the foods given to us, we aim to use their life force to the fullest. Since foods are gifts from nature, we can accept them as they are and, making the most of their color, shape, smell, and taste, create wonderful meals.

These principles apply not only to stalks of vegetable, but to rice and other foods. It has been said that a grain of rice weighs as much as Mount Sumeru. We should take care of each grain of rice and all other foods with love and gentleness, as if we were protecting our own eyes.

Ordinarily, people think a buddha is "a six-foot-tall golden body with thirty-two distinguishing marks and eight different kinds of manifestations." This is how people interpret buddha, because they have a narrow point of view born of strong discrimination between love and hate, right and wrong. With our discriminating mind, we never see the true form of actual reality. We are influenced by the illusions caused by like and dislike, love and hate, and out of that come good and bad, and ugliness and beauty.

If we can see actual reality and accept everything as it is, then everything is fine and nothing is difficult. If we can change our way of thinking, we can see everything as it is: how high the mountain is, how flat the ocean's surface is, how red the flower is, how green the weeping willow is, how blue the mountain ridge is. We can hear the sound of the valley stream as it is. All are revealing their true nature.

Each one has its own truth, the ultimate reality of all things, which is the most valuable jewel of its existence. If we can stand in the world of absolute value and look around, then we can see all things as they are, and they will speak to us. To live in the world of absolute value is the true practice of Buddhism. Understanding "lifting one stalk of vegetable to make a six-foot body of buddha" is turning the great wheel of dharma.

Xuefeng Overturns the Rice Bowl

There is a famous episode in the *Instructions for the Cook* about Xuefeng Yicun (822–908 CE) when he was tenzo under Dongshan Liangjie (807–69). Xuefeng is described there as being tenzo, or head cook, while according to other Zen records he was a rice cook, a subordinate of the tenzo. It does not matter whether he was tenzo or rice cook because both are names of positions in the kitchen and their task is preparing meals for the community.

One day while the rice was being cleaned, Dongshan asked, "Are you sifting the sand and removing the rice, or sifting the rice and removing the sand?"

Xuefeng said, "Sand and rice are simultaneously removed."

Dongshan said, "What will the great assembly eat?"

Xuefeng overturned the bowl.

Dongshan said, "In the future you will go and be scrutinized by someone else."

The last sentence, "In the future you will go and be scrutinized by someone else," was recorded differently in *Rules of Purity for Temple Administrators* (*Chiji Shingi*, another of the texts in *Rules of Purity for Eiheiji*). That version reads, "In accord with your causal conditioning you will later meet Deshan."

Xuefeng is famous for having been tenzo for a long time, in many temples. He studied three times under Touzi and he visited and studied with Dongshan nine times. Finally, Deshan Xuanjian recognized Xuefeng's potential to be a vessel of dharma. Feeling a strong dharma connection, Xuefeng became Deshan's disciple and received his dharma transmission. After the transmission, he lived and practiced dharma at Mount Xuefeng for forty years.[1] The Zen record says that he always had more than fifteen hundred trainees in his assembly, including many excellent disciples who later became famous, like Yunmen Wenyan and Xuansha Shibei.

Zen master Dongshan and practitioner Xuefeng were both very serious about practicing the buddha way. They knew that zazen, dedication, and chanting are not the only practices of the way. When Xuefeng was cleaning rice, that work was his precious practice of the buddha way, and the kitchen was the precious site for practice. Whenever and wherever we are, we are exactly in the midst of Zen practice.

Usually, to clean the rice means to rinse out the sand, the bugs, and the dust with water. When we clean the rice, we should not only pay attention to the sand and bugs, but also to the rice. We must pay attention to everything at the same time: the rice, the sand, the bugs, and the water, mindful not to waste even a single grain of rice.

Dongshan asked Xuefeng, "Are you sifting the sand and removing the rice, or sifting the rice and removing the sand?" This is not a usual question.

When we are fully in the moment of the task with our whole self, mind and body, we do not think about whether we strain the rice or the sand. To clean the rice is to strain out the sand. To clean the sand is to strain out the rice. We cannot separate the jobs, they are done simultaneously.

Is the rice or the sand being cleaned? As soon as we ask this question, we are involved in a dualistic view. In Zen we aim to see the original reality of all beings directly and to view things based on nonduality. When we clean the rice, only rice is there. And when we sift the sand, only the sand is there. There is no duality. The world of nothing-but-rice is there. The world of only-sand is there. So Xuefeng answered, "Sand and rice are simultaneously removed."

When we are sleeping and start dreaming, our sleep is not really deep. When we are sleeping like a log, we do not dream and we don't know whether we are snoring or not. We are simply sleeping without knowing that we are sleeping. As another example, when we put our whole being into our work, we lose track of time and forget ourselves. We even forget what we are doing. However, when a thought like "I am doing something wholeheartedly, forgetting both work and self" arises even for a second, then the work and ourselves become separate. The task and the self are opposed and become as far from each other as heaven is from earth.

Here, Xuefeng does put his whole self into his diligent practice, completely forgetting himself, cleaning the rice. Within the action of cleaning rice, Xuefeng, rice, and sand become unified. The person and the surroundings work together in harmony. "Sand and rice are simultaneously removed" is Xuefeng's natural expression of working wholeheartedly and losing track of time. Xuefeng's attitude as tenzo was that here and now is the place for the practice of buddha dharma.

Xuefeng's response, "Sand and rice are simultaneously removed," may sound like a very good answer. But it is not the end of the story. We can aim to do our best to put our whole self into our practice, but if we are not going in the right direction, it will be like trying to go south by pointing our vehicle north. Therefore, Dongshan continued to question him.

Dongshan's question was, if the sand and the rice disappear at once, what will the practitioners eat? This kind question shows Dongshan's greatness as a teacher. The meaning of this "what" is a very important point.

Instead of answering Dongshan's question using words, Xuefeng overturned the rice pot, giving Dongshan a clear insight into Xuefeng's immaturity.

According to the view of absolute existence, "sand and rice are simultaneously removed" is not wrong. It is not wrong, but Xuefeng ignores that cleaning the rice is for the sake of cooking rice and offering it to the practitioners so they can enjoy a delicious meal. This is also the way to make the best use of the rice. Even though both rice and sand are one and the same existence which has absolute value, if the tenzo were to cook sand instead of rice, the practitioners would not be able to eat. The full potential of the sand is not being utilized either; there must be a different way to use it. For example, when we use cement, sand is very important. If extraneous things like rice get mixed in they have to be removed or else the cement will not set properly.

There is a clear difference between the absolute value of existence and utility value. Dongshan clarified the difference between the two by asking, "If sand and rice are simultaneously removed, then what do we eat?"

Xuefeng could not understand what Dongshan meant. Xuefeng mixed up utility value with absolute value. Furthermore, because Xuefeng was clinging to his understanding of absolute nonduality, he could not work freely.

Dongshan expected in his heart that someday Xuefeng would become a free-minded and great Zen master after practicing with another teacher and getting rid of that sickness. That is why Dongshan said to Xuefeng, "In the future you will go and be scrutinized by someone else." Dongshan was right. Xuefeng became a great Zen teacher and trained many capable disciples.

Dongshan and Three Pounds of Hemp

One day when Dongshan Shouchu (910–90) was tenzo, weighing hemp in the kitchen, a monk asked, "What is buddha?" Dongshan answered, "Three pounds of hemp."

Dongshan Shouchu was Yunmen's disciple. This is a well-known kōan from ancient times. There is another famous kōan, in which Zhaozhou answers the same question saying, "The cypress tree in the garden." When the monk asked, "What is Buddha?" Dongshan replied, "Three pounds of hemp." Why does Buddha become three pounds of hemp? Dongshan was dealing with the hemp wholeheartedly, just like Xuefeng cleaning the rice. He put his entire being into the act of weighing the hemp, concentrating only on weighing it without any distracting thoughts.

As tenzo, we must consider the pot that cooks the rice as our own precious head and the water that cleans the rice as our own precious life force. The hemp is Dongshan. Dongshan is the hemp. The person and the object are one and inseparable. Dongshan is Buddha. Buddha is Dongshan. "Three pounds of hemp" is a natural response for Dongshan.

Xuefeng said, "Sand and rice are simultaneously removed." Dongshan said that Buddha is three pounds of hemp. These statements do not make any sense at all when we only think of the surface meaning of the words. We need to have deep insight into why they made such responses and what they wanted to express through those words, reading between the lines. It is not enough just to understand the meaning of those wonderful daily-life teachings of the ancestral masters. We need to make efforts to adapt their way of conducting themselves into our own practice of the buddha way, thus bringing the kōans to life. Applying the essential truth to our present actions in our day-to-day activities, and thoroughly seeing and embodying it are the great characteristics of Zen practice.

The Kōan Manifests in the Kitchen

Xuefeng's cleaning rice and Dongshan's weighing hemp are only two examples of the practice of the buddha way, which is not the cultivation of special personal qualities through extraordinary activities outside our usual day-to-day lives. The true buddha way lies in doing ordinary things in ordinary ways and living daily life simply and naturally.

This applies to all manner of situations. Beyond the particular job you have, or the place you are in, put your whole self into whatever you are doing right this moment. Wherever you are, do your best. Just be mindful and enjoy working samadhi. No matter what you are doing, watch closely and, with your own hands, do everything with the most sincere diligence. When the king of animals, the lion, tries to catch a small rabbit or a huge giraffe it does not concern itself with whether it is small or big. The lion uses the same approach, using its whole body to catch its prey.

We tend to hand boring duties over to other people, not valuing them. By treating boring jobs lightly, we treat ourselves lightly. "Do not yield a single drop in the ocean of merit; even a mountain of good karma can be augmented by a single particle of dust."

A company president is a president, employees are employees. Teachers are teachers, and homemakers are homemakers. Each job has its own environment and situation, and offers you an opportunity to become aware of your own meaning and existence. If we are not distracted by frustration or complaints, the wisdom of buddha's light will help us recognize our own dignity. We must always try to improve ourselves, by simply doing our best to fulfill our designated roles moment by moment, day after day, finishing up this day's work without postponing it until the next day.

Some may feel demeaned by the tenzo's work, but if we broaden our view and actively put our whole energy into our work, we can find a path to nurture our personality to maturity. Accepting kitchen work as buddha's work, it is easier for us to carry it out with a sincere heart. This helps us learn to find dignity in all work and see the preciousness of our own lives. We can consider our work to be a place where we express our life force fully and freely with joy. At that time the practice of the buddha way will be fulfilled through our body and mind.

If we are homemakers, we have many kinds of jobs to do besides kitchen work; yet even if we are busy, we cannot skip kitchen work for even one day. As soon as breakfast is over, we have to think about lunch. After lunch, planning and preparation for dinner are waiting for us. This is easy if we have plenty of time and a limitless budget, but it takes effort and practice to learn to purchase the freshest food with the least amount of money.

To cook a meal may take two hours, while to eat it may take only five minutes. Often cooking does not receive due credit considering how much effort and time it takes. When we put love into preparing the food, it bears the cook's unique flavor. If we demonstrate this concern to our children, whether the meal is elaborate or simple, the children will perceive the joy and preciousness of kitchen work. The finished product is important, but the process of doing it is even more important. Cooking even simple food for ourselves reminds us how much work it is to prepare meals and helps us to respect and deeply appreciate cooks.

Modern society is moving faster and faster, and we have machines to help with every daily chore. This is convenient, but in our rush we tend to forget the importance of appreciation and graciousness. The desire for quick results with the least labor tends to lead to poor-quality food. If we always eat such foods, we will become poorly produced people. This is terrible. If we do not value the process of work, we cannot cook good food.

When we cook, we should not complain about whether the ingredients are good or bad, plentiful or scanty. Complaining does not solve anything and such discrimination will affect our attitude when we prepare food. First we examine the materials. If the vegetable is fresh, we can eat it raw. If its natural state is too hard, we cook it. Perishable food should be used first. If the quality of the ingredients is bad, we must accept it and work around it. Using what we have with awareness, we must examine the food and figure out the best way to prepare it.

Using rice as an example, we ask, "Is the rice fresh or old, brown rice or white rice, regular or sweet rice? Where was it produced?" We examine the rice and then figure out the best way to prepare it. Should we make gruel or plain rice, rice cake or rice cooked with red beans, tea rice or mixed rice, sushi rice or rice balls? Depending upon the kind of rice and the final product, the amount of cooking water and the cooking process will differ. The other dishes to be served, such as miso soup and the side dishes, will also be determined depending upon the way we cook the rice. We must consider the entire meal before we begin.

When this way of careful and thoughtful cooking and paying close attention to the details comes together harmoniously with the wholehearted attitude of a tenzo, we can work freely. This is how we turn the great dharma wheel.

■ ■ ■

1. As with many other masters, Xuefeng's name comes from the place where he taught. This is not his original dharma name, but it is the name he was and is known by. The source could be the temple's or city's name, or, as in this case, the name of the mountain where his temple was located.

Magnanimous Mind

Kōdō Kurebayashi

Instructions for the Cook, written in 1237, was a relatively early work within Dōgen's overall career. He wrote Bendōwa (Talk on Wholehearted Practice of the Way) which is usually considered the first chapter of the Shōbōgenzō, in 1231, and "Great Perfection of Wisdom"[1] and "Genjō-kōan" (Manifestation of Reality) were written in 1233. Although these important chapters were written before Instructions for the Cook, most of the chapters of the Shōbōgenzō were written after it. Its early provenance is certainly an indication of the importance of its contents in Dōgen's mind, and it is interesting to see how its major themes resonate throughout the rest of his writings, especially in the ninety-five chapters of the Shōbōgenzō.

Magnanimous Mind

Instructions for the Cook begins with the description of the different offices of Zen monastic administration. Although there is no attempt to describe the duties of each office in detail, there is a clear emphasis on the mental attitude involved. In the conclusion to the text, Dōgen writes that all such officers, not only the tenzo, should maintain the three minds: joyful mind, parental or nurturing mind, and magnanimous mind. These three fundamental attitudes of religious practice have been described frequently in writings on Sōtō Zen. Here I will discuss only magnanimous mind, which represents a core teaching of the Sōtō school.

Instructions for the Cook describes magnanimous mind as follows:

> So-called great mind is, in its spirit, like a great mountain or a great sea: it has no partiality and no factionalism. Lifting an ounce, it does not consider it light; hefting a stone, it does not consider it heavy. . . . It views pennyweights and ounces [of silver] within the context of a single system of measurement. As an emblem of this sameness, we can write the character "great."

This is of course a kind of sermon, a religious instruction to Dōgen's students, but it is also one of Dōgen's core teachings. Magnanimous mind, literally "great mind," is not simply breadth of mind, but the "mind that exhausts all the worlds in the ten directions," and thus the focal point of all Buddhist spiritual cultivation. Dōgen wrote that "one should write the character 'great,' understand the character 'great,' and study the character 'great.'" According to him, it was in this manner that all the previous great spiritual masters accomplished success in the "one great matter of causes and conditions (of life)."

"Mind that exhausts all the worlds in the ten directions" is a commonly used phrase in Zen texts. It means to see all in one, to grasp the eternal in the moment, and to unite all heaven and earth in the self. This is not simply a form of philosophical idealism, since all things are interconnected without limit. The universe exists on the basis of the self in the here-and-now. These are ideas basic to Zen, and basic to Buddhism in general. It is on this basis that *Instructions for the Cook* urges one to correctly grasp the present moment and be aware of the absolute greatness of one's present self and ranks the role of tenzo as the highest form of the religious life.

This emphasis might seem to be a kind of self-intoxication or delusion, but to embrace within oneself all the worlds in the ten directions, the entire great earth and empty sky, is a fundamental attitude of being a Buddhist and a basic concept of Buddhism. Without this attitude and view, the buddha dharma does not make sense. Dōgen addressed this in the *Shōbōgenzō* chapter "Only Buddha and Buddha," saying, "The practice of buddha takes place in the company of the entire great earth and all sentient beings. Practice that does not exhaust all is not that of buddha." At first this would seem to mean that the actions of one's training take place throughout all the worlds in all directions. However, with further thought we may understand Dōgen's meaning to be that the work of the self is the work of all those worlds in all directions. The

Shōbōgenzō chapter "Studying the Way with Body and Mind" states, "Going-and-coming, with the whole Universe in the ten directions as two wings or three wings, goes flying away and comes flying back, and with the whole Universe in the ten directions as three feet or five feet, steps forward and steps backward."[1]

This means that even though human actions seem to be a matter of individual action, we actually function with heaven and earth, together bearing the entire universe. This is essentially the same idea as the multi-level interdependency described in the *Flower Garland Sutra*. But the phrasing in the "Only Buddha and Buddha" chapter is fresh and startling. We must remember, as we examine the other basic ideas of *Instructions for the Cook*, that the practice and study of the character "great" has a profound significance that is repeated in various forms throughout Dōgen's writings.

Mind in Shōbōgenzō

Since to transcribe, study, and understand the "magnanimous mind" requires a mind, we should consider exactly how this concept is used in *Instructions for the Cook*. In Japanese the Chinese character in question can be pronounced either *shin* or *kokoro*, but the latter includes a wide range of nuances related to human emotions. Here "mind" refers to the mental ability to perceive and distinguish subject and objects, here and there, and self and others, so the reading *kokoro* is not appropriate. Of course, in Dōgen's usage "mind" is something so broad as to far surpass self and others, and all other distinctions.

In Buddhism the mind that perceives and evaluates objects is called the discriminating mind. This universal feature of human life makes us selfish and difficult to control, and conflict and fighting are an unavoidable consequence. The Buddha regretted this and regarded peace and harmony as the ideal. Buddhists are those who work to make this ideal a reality in the present world, and their natural tendency is to attempt to attain that ideal themselves and help others to reach it as well. The goal is to replace the fighting mind with the cooperative mind, the tainted mind with the pure mind, and the small mind with the great or magnanimous mind.

This is an important point. If our minds were definitively tainted, it would be impossible to transform them no matter how hard we tried. Buddhism regards our original human nature as pure and suggests that we work not to lose that original purity. From a perspective that knows purity and taint, our fundamental nature is the pure mind. However, from the perspective in which there is no distinction between self and others, ours is a "magnanimous mind" of limitless breadth.

In this human world where struggle is a constant fact of life, there are borders everywhere, national territoriality on both land and sea. Humans are aggressive toward each other. In the world of the buddhas, where all confrontation is overcome, there is no way to fight. Shakyamuni Buddha contemplated the cause of human conflict and the manner of its transcendence, and Dōgen did so as well. The depth of their insights cannot be achieved by most people, but it is attainable by those who undertake lives of profound cultivation. The "mind" posited in the *Shōbōgenzō* is just such a profound insight, which is why it is called "true mind" (*shinjin*).

Mind in the Chapter "Mind Is Buddha"

Many of the chapters of the *Shōbōgenzō* discuss mind. The eleven most important of these are "Mind Is Buddha," "Mind Unattainable," "Mind Unattainable (second version)," "Studying the Way with Body and Mind," "Mind of the Ancient Buddha," "The Three Worlds Are Only Mind," "Expressing Mind, Expressing Nature," "Generating the Insurpassable Mind," "Generating the Mind of Enlightenment," "Penetrating the Minds of Others," and "Mind of the Way."

These texts all consider the original, pure mind that exists underneath the tainted minds of our ordinary daily activities. The necessary functions of thinking and discrimination are something like clouds, which cover the true mind and make it normally invisible to us. Dōgen's emphasis in these texts is to have us become aware of the fundamental good that we have inherited as human beings. His point is not to have us attempt to attain purity by abandoning that which is defiled, nor to have us transform our delusions into enlightenment in meditation. This is a fundamental religious position within the Sōtō Zen school.

For example, the concept of this mind being the buddha (*sokushin zebutsu*) has a long history within Zen. We also see the phrase "this body is the Buddha" (*sokushin zebutsu*; though homophones, the two characters pronounced *shin* are different). A person who is disciplined and without confusion both within and without may certainly be considered a buddha. The earliest Zen teacher to emphasize the identity of mind and buddha was Mazu Daoyi (709-88). At times he also asserted "neither mind, nor buddha," just to create a useful sort of confusion in his students' minds. That is, if both body and mind are truly refined and under control, they cannot be called anything, even buddha. Hence it is incorrect to understand Mazu's negation as implying that "even buddha is useless."

For Dōgen, the mind Mazu was talking about in his equation of mind and buddha must have been that of the "magnanimous mind." The proof for this is in his chapter "Mind Is Buddha," where he presents this topic in terms of the myriad dharmas or things of this world: "The mind which has been correctly transmitted [in the Zen lineage] is the one mind which is identical to all the dharmas, the dharmas which are all the one mind. Therefore an ancient teacher said, 'If one understands mind, there is not an inch of dirt in the great earth, know that when mind is understood, the canopy of heaven collapses and the earth that surrounds us crumbles.'"

Here Dōgen writes in terms of understanding rather than controlling the mind. This usage is equivalent to the study of the magnanimous mind discussed in the *Instructions for the Cook*. In both cases, if everything is organically connected the enlightenment of human beings is expressed as the equivalence of the one mind and all dharmas, and neither mountains nor rivers stand outside of the framework of this one mind. The great earth does not exist, nor even a single inch of dirt. The heaven or sky above us is also not heaven, the earth is not earth, and everything returns to the one mind that exhausts all the realms of existence. If that one mind is referred to as buddha, then this mind is buddha.

Mind in the Chapter "Mind Unattainable"

The chapter "Mind Unattainable" examines the magnanimous mind and its imperceptibility from a different perspective.

The *Diamond Sutra*, the full title of which is *Sutra of the Perfection of Wisdom That Cuts Even Diamond*, includes the line, "Past mind is unattainable, present mind is unattainable, future mind is unattainable." For convenience this is referred to as the "mind that is unattainable in the three periods." The usual understanding of the phrase "unattainable" (*fukatoku*) here is "impossible to grasp," with the past mind already departed and thus beyond reach, the present mind too evanescent in its transition to the past, and the future mind not yet arrived. The thoroughgoing impermanence of the ceaseless flow of time is a basic fact of our lives. Comprehension of this impermanence is achieved only by a very few people. Another *Shōbōgenzō* chapter, "Total Actualization," treats this issue in terms of being enlightened to the manifestation of total actualization, but here, in "Mind Unattainable," the same issue is handled from the perspective of the magnanimous mind. That is, past, present, and future are handled as three aspects of mind, the understanding of which is identical to the study of magnanimous mind as described in the *Instructions for the Cook*.

In "Mind Unattainable" Dōgen explains that mind is limitless and universal, and that it transcends time. Hence "unattainable" has two mutually contradictory meanings. One is the imperceptibility of the mind that is always in motion, flowing like a never-ending river. The other is the absence of all the things of this world, which ultimately cannot be measured or perceived in subject-object terms. These interpretations are completely opposite to each other, but most people appreciate only the latter, that things cannot be grasped with the mind. The story of Deshan, who was a disciple of Longtan, demonstrates this well.

Before becoming a Zen practitioner, Deshan was a scholar who specialized in the study of the *Diamond Sutra*. Having studied a large number of commentaries on the text, he naturally was aware of the Southern Chan school's position regarding the transmission of Buddhism outside the teachings. Angered by this rejection of doctrinal study, he set out, with his commentaries in hand, to go defeat the Chan arguments in face-to-face debate.

On the way, as he was hiking up a mountain pass, Deshan became hungry and stopped at a tea shop. An old woman was selling rice cakes, and he asked for one. In response, the old woman asked what he was carrying. He told her he had commentaries on the *Diamond Sutra* with him, and he bragged that as the world's greatest authority on the text he would be happy to teach it to her if she was interested. The woman replied that she had studied the text a little and knew of the phrase "Past mind is unattainable, present mind is unattainable, future mind is unattainable." She asked Deshan, "With which unattainable mind are you going to eat the rice cake?"

Deshan could not answer. The woman refused to sell him any cakes and proceeded to simply ignore him. For him, the rice cake was literally unattainable, and he had failed in the simple task of getting something to eat!

Dōgen criticized both Deshan and the old woman for not understanding the true meaning of mind and the buddha way. Both understood "unattainable" too literally. He felt that the woman should have picked up three rice cakes and thrown them at Deshan saying, "This first rice cake is a past mind that is unattainable, this second rice cake is a present mind that is unattainable, and this third rice cake is a future mind that is unattainable!" If she had done something like this she would have been a great master, but she only looked away. She had not understood unattainability at all.

Dōgen's understanding of the one mind as limitless, universal, and all-inclusive may be a type of monism or idealism, but it is different from the way such systems are usually presented.

Magnanimous Mind in the Chapter "Eyeball"

The very heart of Dōgen's teaching in *Instructions for the Cook* (he actually refers to it as the "pupil" of the eye of the true Dharma) is frugality with regard to the common property of the monastic community. There is a sharp contrast between Dōgen's emphasis on this frugality and the values of contemporary consumer society. Where nowadays consumption has become a positive value, for Buddhists it represents nothing less than suicide, the loss of one's own authenticity. But Dōgen's frugality exists on a different level than the commonplace virtue. When he writes that one should be frugal with regard to the monastery's supplies, he is taking the perspective of the oneness of subject and object, the identity of oneself with the myriad things of this world. Those myriad things are oneself, one's own flesh and blood, so that to use them up is to exhaust one's own skin and bones. Given the profound realization that "all the realms in the ten directions of space are one's own body," one must avoid taking things lightly. One must treat the myriad things of existence with care and focused attention.

When Dōgen tells us to treat the monastery's possessions "as if they were one's own eyeballs," he is not referring to one's ordinary eyes but rather to the "buddha eye" that correctly discriminates and understands all matters. Dōgen is making a profound religious assertion.

The buddha eye sees all things in their intimate mutual relationships, and therefore recognizes the absolute value possessed by each and every thing. This capability is of a different quantum level of significance from the seeing of the ordinary human eye, but Buddhism holds that every human being possesses just this buddha eye. In the "Eyeball" chapter of the *Shōbōgenzō* Dōgen refers to the "single eye of the monk that exhausts all the realms in the ten directions." That "single eye" is the only one in the entire universe, and it is not disposed to the errors of accepting, rejecting, and becoming attached to the individual things it sees. It is the eye that sees the entirety of space as a single thing, that sees all interdependences from the time before they became intertwined. It is the same as the magnanimous mind discussed above.

Although everyone possesses it from birth, since it must be refined through long study and practice it is referred to as the "buddha eye." Zen texts refer to "losing the eyes." The meaning of this latter term is that one is to discard one's ordinary eyes, or transform them into the buddha eye, another way of saying one should open one's eyes in awakening.

Dōgen's teacher Rujing says the following about "losing the eye":

Six years lost in the forest with the wild fox spirit.
To escape this impure body—this is the dilemma.
Losing one's eye, unable to find it anywhere,
one deludes people by saying, "Enlightened at the Vaishakha star."

When Gautama lost his eyes,
there was only a single plum flower in the snow.
Now it's become brambles everywhere,
blooming all over, laughing instead at the spring breeze.

Here Dōgen's teacher Rujing, the abbot of Jingde Monastery at Mount Tiantong, taught his followers using the example of Shakyamuni's enlightenment. His uniquely Zen style of expression seems to break through the very meaning of his words. Even now Zen teachers make ironic references to Shakyamuni as the "wild fox spirit" who "deludes people," but at the same time they also speak of "losing the eye." "Losing the eye" is used to describe not the inability to see things normally but the dismissal of the ordinary way of seeing things. Rujing is saying that the Buddha's enlightenment was a misrepresentation, because people are not originally ignorant, that the Buddha's enlightenment was originally overshadowed by a single plum flower blossoming in the snow, and that this scene would eventually evolve into the luxuriant splendor of springtime. Everything returns to the one, and the one evolves into everything: this is the enlightenment of the Buddha. Without losing one's ordinary eye, one cannot attain the "single eye of the monk that exhausts all the realms in the ten directions."

Magnanimous Mind in the Chapter "Kannon"

There are no references to Kannon, or Avalokiteshvara Bodhisattva, in *Instructions for the Cook*, but the colophon at the beginning of the text reads, "By the monk Dōgen of the Kannon Dōri Kōshō Hōrin Zen Monastery," and at the end of the text, "Recorded by the dharma-transmitting monk Dōgen, abbot of the Kannon Dōri Kōshō Hōrin Zen Monastery."

Dōgen was actually deeply interested in Kannon, but not in the ordinary sense of faith in the bodhisattva. What he was impressed with was Kannon's ways of practice: seeing deeply and accepting everything in the world as it is. After Dōgen finished his studies in China and embarked for Japan, the ship Dōgen was on encountered fierce seasonal winds, during which he sat in quiet contemplation. Soon he witnessed Kannon floating above the water on a lotus blossom, at which point the storm immediately subsided. After landing safely he built a temple named Kannonji and donated a sculpted image of the "single blossom Kannon" to it.[2] All of this implies that Dōgen's faith in Kannon was similar to that shared by many of his contemporaries. The inscription on this image reads:

> A single flower opens into five petals.
> On each petal is a tathagata.
> With great vows as deep as the ocean,
> I use the excellent material of this statue to return your favor.

I do not have the technical expertise to determine whether or not Dōgen himself wrote this inscription, but it would not be surprising for a Zen monk such as him to have done so. Both Nanyue Huairang and Zhaozhou Congshen lived in Guanyin temples, for example. But what is the connection between Dōgen's faith in Kannon and the "magnanimous mind" described in *Instructions for the Cook*?

The "Kannon" chapter of the *Shōbōgenzō* is devoted to a dispute between Yunyan and Daowu about Kannon, which begins with an allusion to the bodhisattva's thousand arms and eyes.

> Yunyan asked Daowu, "What does the great bodhisattva of compassion do with all those hands?"
> Daowu said, "It's like searching for one's pillow during the night."
> Yunyan said, "I understand, I understand."
> Daowu said, "What do you understand?"
> Yunyan said, "The bodhisattva has hands and eyes all over his body."
> Daowu said, "What you say is outrageous! You've only got eighty or ninety percent of it."
> Yunyan said, "If I'm only that good, what about you?"
> Daowu said, "The bodhisattva's entire body is hands and eyes."

Kannon's thousand hands and eyes are meant to symbolize his great compassion. There may not be much difference between having hands and eyes "all over his body" versus those hands and eyes being his "entire body," both of which are meant to symbolize the bodhisattva's nondiscriminating great compassion. Nighttime is no doubt symbolic of the darkness of ignorance, which is also nondiscriminating in its all-enveloping quality. In the dark, not even Kannon can tell who he is helping—and this is precisely the "magnanimous mind" of *Instructions for the Cook*. Kannon's body fills all the realms of the ten directions; this is the locus of the teaching, the scale of great compassion. Therefore, in the Zen tradition faith in Kannon occurs on the foundation of the "study of the character 'great' (or 'magnanimous')," and we must approach Dōgen's faith from this perspective.

The other chapter of the *Shōbōgenzō* that discusses Kannon is "Great Perfection of Wisdom." Here the bodhisattva is referred to by the name Kanjizai, meaning "he who sees autonomously." Kannon and Kanjizai are identical, but the former emphasizes his compassion and the latter his wisdom. Sometimes we are so devoted to the Kannon of compassion that we overlook the Kanjizai of wisdom, but the widespread use of the *Heart Sutra* throughout Japanese Buddhism helps keep this aspect of his identity in the foreground.

The great wisdom of Kanjizai is that all the dharmas are empty, everything is empty. Even if we repeatedly chant the *Heart Sutra*, if we don't accept the wisdom for our own, we are like the son who wandered away from his father's palace in the famous parable from the *Lotus Sutra*. It is a great contradiction if we recite the *Heart Sutra* that emphasizes emptiness and wish to gain some benefit that is not empty.

We can begin to develop magnanimous mind by studying "the character 'great,'" as Dōgen recommends. Throughout the day and night, we can continue to investigate magnanimous mind in all our daily activities, learning to drop the scales of discrimination from our eyes, finally "losing our eyes" altogether. Then we can function smoothly in every moment, realizing the limitless quality of our activities.

■ ■ ■

1   This quotation is from "Master Dōgen's Shōbōgenzō Book 2," p. 256, translated by Gudō Nishijima & Chodo Cross, Windbell Publication, London, 1996.
2   This story appears in Menzan Zuiho's notes for *Kenzeiki*, the Dōgen biography written by the fourteenth abbot of Eiheiji, Kenzei.

Just Cooking, Just Sitting

Kōshō Uchiyama

There is a story at the beginning of the *Pure Standards for Temple Administrators* (*Chiji Shingi*, one of the essays in Zen Master Dōgen's *Rules of Purity for Eiheiji*, or *Eihei Shingi*), about Master Wuzhuo Wenxi when he was tenzo at Mount Wutai.[1] One day while he was cooking rice gruel, Manjushri suddenly appeared above the rice pot. Manjushri is the bodhisattva of wisdom enshrined at the center of the monks' hall, and he is believed to reside at Mount Wutai, in the far north of China. When Wuzhuo saw the bodhisattva he hit him and declared, "Even if Shakyamuni Buddha showed up here, I would hit him."

I was ordained as a Sōtō Zen monk on December 8, 1941, by Kōdō Sawaki Roshi, the very day World War II began in the Pacific.[2] After my ordination, my early days of practice were miserable because it was wartime. After the war was over in 1945, my life settled down a little and practitioners gathered together under Sawaki Roshi. Gradually we formed a zazen practice community at Antaiji, in Kyoto. However, in 1948 and 1949, even though I had already been a monk for seven or eight years, I couldn't clarify the essential point of zazen practice at all. I was profoundly troubled in mind during those days. In addition to this, we had a food shortage. We lived at a starvation level in Japan that people in the developed countries today simply can't imagine. In those days, when I was assigned the duty of tenzo, I could sneak extra food for myself. I thought that was the only benefit of being a tenzo.

But when I worked as tenzo in the kitchen with such a secretive and underhanded spirit, I discovered that there was something haphazard in my work. Not only when I was thinking about snitching a little food, but even when I was thinking about zazen and trying to clarify its meaning, I made careless mistakes in my work as tenzo. During the war, I hadn't had any spare time to study the *Rules of Purity for Eiheiji* to illuminate my mind with the ancient teachings. In those postwar days, I had a little time to spare for study, and when I read this story of Zen Master Wuzhuo it struck home. I realized that it applied to me too: when I was cooking rice gruel, even if Manjushri were to appear and try to grab some, I should hit him and chase him away and just continue straightforwardly to cook. If Manjushri or a hungry ghost were to appear above the rice pot, I would not be a true practitioner if I could not break the illusion. I reflected deeply on this point and from then on I made an effort to work as tenzo without the spirit of dishonesty or of using my position for my personal advantage.

Dōgen says, "The buddha dharma correctly transmitted through buddhas and ancestors is just sitting (*shikantaza*)." Zazen is the most important practice in his teachings, but in the *Instructions for the Cook* he also says that the tenzo's work is the most important practice. He says, "Among the myriad dharmas, the most revered and precious are the three jewels. Now we have the good fortune to be born as a human being and to prepare food that these three jewels receive and use. Is this not of great karmic significance? We should thus be very happy." Therefore, he concludes, "When you prepare food and cook it you should do so with the aspiration of taking tens of thousands of births and concentrating them into this one day, this one time, that you may be able to bind together in good karmic result the bodies of millions of [past] births."

Should we be doing both at once, thinking about tenzo affairs while we are sitting in zazen and thinking about zazen while working as a tenzo? Is this better than simply sitting or simply cooking? It does not work that way. We should just sit when we do zazen (*shikan taza*) and when we do the tenzo's work we should just work as the tenzo (*shikan tenzo*). Then the common thing in both practices is the attitude toward life that is "just" (*shikan*). This attitude of "just"—or "nothing but," or perhaps "undivided"— is the foundation of Dōgen's teachings. What is the significance of this attitude of "just" for our way of life

Just Sitting

I want to examine the relationship between the tenzo's work and just sitting (*shikantaza*). *Instructions for the Cook* gives us a clear explanation of the tenzo's work. But, when we look into shikantaza, even though there are many texts we can refer to, there is no particular text in which Dōgen precisely addresses shikantaza. This is a problem for us, so I would like to discuss the shikantaza taught by Dōgen according to my understanding and then look at its relationship to *Instructions for the Cook*.

Shikantaza means to just and solely sit. But what do we actually do in zazen? Dōgen calls zazen "the samadhi that is the king of samadhis" (*zanmai-ō-zanmai*), so our zazen has something to do with "samadhi." "Samadhi" is translated into Chinese as *tōji* (holding all things equally) or *shinikkyōshō* (focusing the mind on a single object, or embracing dharma in the unity of mind and each single object).

The word "mind" (*shin*) is a problem, and depending on how we understand it, the way we practice zazen varies. First, "mind" is commonly interpreted as psychological mind or consciousness (*citta*). If we understand "mind" in this sense, "focusing the mind on a single object" means to put all the distracting threads of our minds together and focus them on one object. In that case zazen is concentrating the mind, or a method of training to become no-mind and no-thought, to empty the mind of all thoughts. Non-Buddhist meditation practice and early Buddhist meditation practices are such methods of discipline.[3]

Our minds are almost always distracted; the practitioner uses such practices to try to pacify the floating mind and make it harmonious. It is clear, however, that Dōgen's zazen is not a discipline for putting one's mind under one's control. Dōgen says, "A Buddha ancestor said that it is better to have the mind of a wily fox than to follow a narrow way of self-regulation."[4]

"Mind" is sometimes used as a Buddhist term in this sense of psychological mind or consciousness, but it is more commonly used with a different meaning, as when Dōgen says, "The mind that has been correctly transmitted is that of 'one mind is all dharmas' and 'all dharmas are one mind.'"[5]

It is obvious that this "mind" does not refer to psychological mind or consciousness, as in the common usage. But "the mind that has been correctly transmitted" is nothing other than this "one mind is all dharmas and all dharmas are one mind." In this sense our zazen of mind focused on one object is mind and object unified, and not at all a method of discipline for concentration or for training to become no-mind and no-thought, as people usually think.

What does this expression "one mind is all dharmas and all dharmas are one mind" mean? Buddhism has been refined by generation after generation of ancestors since it originated with Shakyamuni Buddha in India. When Buddhism uses even a simple word, it gradually develops a profound and decisive meaning instead of a merely relative meaning. In the case of "mind," it was originally used in the sense of psychological mind, but when it is used in an expression like "one mind is all dharmas and all dharmas are one mind," its meaning has been thoroughly deepened and it is used in an absolute sense.

How was it deepened? When we live, we are together with the world in which we are living. More concretely speaking, we usually think that this world exists before we were born, and our entrance into this already existing world we call our birth. Dying then means we exit from this actually existing world, and even after we die, this world exists as reality. However, when we think this way, we have already reified concepts. This is not reality itself, it is an idea about it. The concrete world that is reality itself, in which I actually dwell and actually live my real experience, cannot possibly be such a conceptual and abstract world.

For example, suppose that you and I are looking at a tea bowl. We assume we are looking at the same tea bowl, yet, in reality that is not the case. You are looking at the tea bowl from your angle with your own eyes through the conditions of sunlight from your side. I am looking at the tea bowl from my angle, with my eyes, in the conditions of sunlight from my side. We roughly abstract it and identify it and conceptually create "the same tea bowl." This is the way we reify concepts.

In the same way, we simply assume that the world in which you and I and all other people are living and experiencing life exists and is one and the same world, although this is nothing other than the reification of concepts. Not only that, we believe we are born, live, and die in this world of reified concepts; this really is an upside-down way of viewing things.

The world of reality in which this true self of mine actually dwells and actually experiences life is the world only this self can experience. This world of mine cannot be exchanged with the worlds of others. Even a fart cannot be given or received from others, in the world of the reality of life. I was born with the world I experience and I am living with the world I experience and I will die with the world I experience.

Thus, on the ground of the reality of the world of my experience, my experience (mind) and reality (the world and objects) are completely one. We can never abstractly separate these two. And yet, if we conclude that everything is dependent upon our mind, we succumb to idealism, and if we conclude on the other hand that our mind is completely dependent on circumstances, we succumb to naive objectivism. Buddhism is clearly neither a rough idealism nor a primitive externalism.

As buddha dharma, we should accept this "mind that is correctly transmitted" as "one mind is all dharmas" and "all dharmas are one mind." After all, what I experience (mind) is the entire world of reality (all dharmas), and the entire world of reality (all dharmas) is nothing other than my experience (mind). Such a usage of the word "mind" does not imply psychological mind but something like "pure life." In living out life, I encounter the world in which I have life-experience. In encountering the world of life-experience, I live out this life.

When "mind" is used in such a sense, what does "embracing dharma within mind and object" mean? It means that we accept everything on the ground of pure life-experience. This is different from our usual approach to life, in which we are constantly creating concepts in our minds and reifying these concepts, and then throwing ourselves into the world of reified concepts and living in that abstraction. "Embracing dharma within mind and object" means that we accept everything in the world (all dharmas) on the ground of our own life-experience (mind) and see everything in the world as the scenery of our own life-experience. *Tōji*, or "holding things equally," another translation of samadhi, means the same thing.

Therefore, if we think we should eliminate the thoughts that arise as we practice zazen, we are not practicing the zazen taught by Dōgen. It is clear that if we chase after thoughts that spring up in our minds and go on pursuing them, we are not doing zazen at all, we are merely thinking. And yet, if we try to eliminate thought, that is one more mental activity; it is a further thought, and it is not zazen either. Zazen as "mind and object are one" is to put everything on the ground of pure life and to open our hand of thought: We neither chase after thoughts nor try to get rid of them, but let them come up freely and disappear freely. We view things as the scenery of the reality of life. This is what Dōgen means when he says in the *Fukan Zazengi* (*Universal Recommendations for Zazen*), "Let go of all associations, and put all affairs aside. Do not think of either good or evil. Do not be concerned with either right or wrong. Put aside the operation of your intellect, volition, and consciousness. Stop considering things with your memory, imagination, and contemplation. Do not seek to become a buddha."

We human beings are living beings with brains. It is completely natural that even when we practice zazen, thoughts arise and pass away. They are, in a sense, a secretion of our brain. And yet, we generally reify these thought secretions, throw ourselves into them, and are imprisoned in this upside-down way of living and thus lose our freedom. On the contrary, what is most important in zazen is to just let secretions be secretions, without being caught up in them, and to keep opening our mental "hands" to let go of thought. Then everything becomes simply the scenery of life (the scenery of the original ground). This is why it is called Zen, a transliteration of the Sanskrit *dhyana*, which literally means "quiet thinking."

The well-known statement by Zen Master Shitou Xiqian that "the vast sky does not obstruct the white clouds from floating freely" expresses this scenery. Our zazen in the Sōtō lineage is called silent illumination Zen because in this zazen we just quietly illuminate everything.[6]

The basis of this silent illumination is that when we sit in zazen, we leave everything to the zazen that is the posture of opening the hand of thought, completely without any mental fabrication. This is what is called just sitting, shikantaza. At such a time, there is no mental activity such as "I want to attain satori," "I want to develop my energy," or " I want to improve my state of mind." Dōgen says in the *Shōbōgenzō Zuimonki* (*Sayings of Dōgen*), "Sitting is nothing other than buddha's practice. Sitting is nondoing. This is itself the true form of the self. There is nothing to seek as buddha dharma beside this sitting."

However, when we start to sleep or think during zazen, if we continue to sleep, that is being out of touch due to sleepiness (*konchin*, dullness or depression), while if we chase after thinking, that is being out of touch due to thinking (*sanran*, distraction). Both dullness and distraction cause us to be out of touch with the reality of pure life. We need to wake up vigorously and keep the posture of zazen. This is most important. Thus, to keep the posture of zazen vigorously with this body is shikantaza (just sitting).

This practice is at the same time enlightenment. We just practice this enlightenment.

Just Cooking

Dōgen's teaching in *Instructions for the Cook* is consistent with this understanding of shikantaza as the attitude that lives out the reality of pure life. He teaches that the way a tenzo works is by practicing the attitude that lives out the reality of pure life in our daily lives. As I said before, we usually reify concepts carelessly and lose sight of reality. *Instructions for the Cook* teaches us that we should first thoroughly destroy our reified concepts and then live and work on the ground of the reality of life.

At the very beginning of *Instructions for the Cook*, Dōgen emphasized the importance of the role of tenzo, destroying the preconceived idea that the work of the tenzo is the same as that of "usual worldly cooks and even the imperial cooks." And he says that "all monastery administrators are buddha's children and together they carry out buddha's work." This means that the tenzo's work is the "single color of diligently engaging in the Way." This is completely different from worldly preconceptions or systems of value, which are based on turning concepts into solid things. We need to destroy such worldly systems of value and practice the attitude that we live in the world of value based on the reality of the life of the self.

I practiced as a tenzo in the assembly under Kōdō Sawaki for a long time. During those years, I copied many extracts of important passages of *Instructions for the Cook* in my notebook to serve as my own guidelines and I kept them by me day and night. A few passages on not separating your life from your work follow, with explanations according to my own understanding. I offer these comments specifically for the sake of those who practice as tenzo and those who want to use Dōgen's *Instructions* as a guideline for other work.[7]

> When ordinarily preparing ingredients, do not regard them with ordinary [deluded] eyes, or think of them with ordinary emotions. "Lifting a single blade of grass builds a shrine, entering a single mote of dust turns the great wheel of the dharma." Even when, for example, one makes a soup of the crudest greens, one should not give rise to a mind that loathes it or takes it lightly; and even when one makes a soup of the finest cream, one should not give rise to a mind that feels glad and rejoices in it.

When Dōgen says "ordinary eyes" and common sentiments, he refers to the eyes and human attitudes that see things with a worldly, preexisting value system. Instead of such common views, we should see both coarse green soup and high-quality cream soup equally and encounter both with an equal attitude, and we should work as if to erect a great temple building for a buddha with one stalk of an ordinary green vegetable. In the same way, when we meet with people, we should not change our attitude depending upon whether the person has high or low social status, or whether the person has a lot of money or not. As practitioners of the buddha way we should not change our attitude based on a worldly viewpoint. I think this is a particularly important teaching.

> As for the [proper] attitude in preparing food offerings and handling ingredients, do not debate the fineness of things and do not debate their coarseness, but take as essential the profound arousal of a true mind and a respectful mind. . . .

> When you select and serve up crude greens, if you do so with a true mind, a sincere mind, and a pure mind, then they will be comparable to superb delicacies. Why is that so? Because when one enters into the pure and vast oceanic assembly of the buddha dharma, superb delicacies are never seen and the flavor of crude greens does not exist: there is only the one taste of the great sea, and that is all.

The fundamental attitude needed to go beyond worldly systems of value is that practitioners live on the ground of the reality of life. We should keep working with actual things, with true mind. Dōgen repeatedly expresses this as "with sincere diligence" or "just prepare sincerely."

To work on the ground of the reality of life is, first of all, to meet things as they really are, with a truly sincere attitude. We do the zazen of "things and mind are one" or "self and others are one," and we work as hard as possible with our heart penetrating all things. To do this we also have to calculate and to make distinctions while we stand on the ground of the reality of life. Early in *Instructions for the Cook*, describing the keen attention the tenzo must give to each detail of meal preparation, Dōgen says, "During the day and through the night, whether things come and dwell in your mind or your mind turns and dwells on things, put yourself on a par with them and diligently engage the way."

I think this is the essential spirit that penetrates the entirety of the teachings in *Instructions for the Cook*. I have often expressed this as " whatever we encounter is our life." This is the fundamental attitude of "just," or shikan. As the reality of life, we are each born together with our own world, we live together with this world and we will die together with this world. We should meet with this world (things) as our life (mind).

This is the attitude Dōgen is expressing when he says, "There are fools who look upon themselves as if they were someone else, and there are wise people who regard others as themselves." Shakyamuni Buddha said, "The triple world is my dwelling and all the living beings there are my children." Within the tenzo's work and in our daily activities, we actually practice this attitude instead of just understanding it as a concept.

"One should maintain a way-seeking mind, make adjustments in accord with the occasion, and see to it that the great assembly receives what is necessary and is at ease." In this way, a tenzo should pay attention to all aspects of meal preparation, put things in order, and make changes to introduce variety. The tenzo's work is to create harmony by putting things where they are best suited, some up high and some down low. With the spirit of making an offering to others, a tenzo should often change the menu and enable all practitioners in the community to practice with pleasure.

Practice with Your Own Body and Mind

Seeing the reality of life, work according to the reality of life. This is the practice of a person in the duty of tenzo. This is the way we practice the true one-flavor Zen that is called "just." I have been discussing the relationship between shikantaza, just sitting, and *Instructions for the Cook* as the process of my own practice of living out the reality of my own life. However, if what I have discussed here becomes mere theory, doctrine, or ideology, without doubt it is no longer the reality of life. Both zazen and tenzo duties should be practiced with our own actual body. There is no other way to carry out either activity.

Dōgen addresses this in one of his teachings in the *Shōbōgenzō Zuimonki* (2-26), saying:

> As long as we only think about the buddha dharma with our minds, the Way will never be grasped, even in a thousand lifetimes or myriad eons. When we let go of our minds and cast aside our views and understandings, the Way will be actualized. . . . Therefore, when we completely cast aside our thoughts and views and practice shikantaza, we will become intimate with the Way. For this reason, the Way is without doubt attained through the body. This is why I encourage you to practice zazen wholeheartedly.

It is exactly the same for the tenzo, for whom "rolling up the sleeves is the mind of the Way." This is a fundamental point. When you sit, just sit. When you are tenzo, just be the tenzo. This is the attitude of "just" or shikan taught by Dōgen. This is to practice the reality of life of the self right now.

■ ■ ■

1 Wuzhuo Wenxi (821–900) was a dharma heir of Yangshan (807–83). Mount Wutai (J., Godaisan), the "five-terraced mountain," is said to be the abode of Manjushri, and many Buddhists have reported visions of him there.
2 Because of the international date line, the attack on Pearl Harbor occurred on December 8, 1941, in Japan, rather than on December 7, as in the West.

3   The word Hinayana is not used by Uchiyama or by Dōgen to refer to any particular tradition of Buddhism. The word refers instead to a narrow attitude toward practice and realization. The term was coined by and the idea was much criticized by early Mahayana Buddhists.

4   *Eihei Kōroku*, The Extensive Record of Eihei Dōgen, a collection of Dōgen's formal speeches, volume 5.

5   *Shōbōgenzō*, "Mind Itself Is Buddha" (Sokushin Zebutsu).

6   Silent Illumination Zen is a translation for *mokushō* Zen. Hongzhi Zhengjue (Wanshi Shōgaku), a well-known Chinese Sōtō Zen Master wrote a piece titled Mokushōmei (Essay on Silent Illumination), in which he described zazen practice in the Sōtō tradition as silent illumination. Dōgen respected Wanshi, but there is some scholarly dispute as to whether Dōgen criticized Wanshi's "silent illumination Zen" or considered it completely the same as his own practice.

7   I have also written a longer commentary on the whole of *Instructions for the Cook*, called From the *Zen Kitchen to Enlightenment* (New York: Weatherhill, 1993). The original Japanese volume for that translation was called "How to Cook Your Life" (Jinsei Ryōri no Hon).

PART III

Roots of Mealtime Practice

Eating Customs in the Early Sangha in India

Kōgen Mizuno

In the first centuries of Indian Buddhism, long before the dharma spread to East Asia and the West, there were no settled, year-round monastic communities. Monks and nuns wandered and taught, truly homeless. They went out every day to beg and received cooked food from their donors. Even when they gathered in seasonal monasteries for long retreats during the annual rainy period, there were no cooking duties, because the monks and nuns still lived on donations of prepared food.

These early monasteries and customs were very different from those described many centuries later by Dōgen, and in particular there was no need for a tenzo. On the surface their food-related practices have almost nothing in common, but on a deeper level their attitudes toward food are consistent. Even in the early period monks had not only to eat to sustain their lives but also to make choices about what to eat, and how and when, and someone had to provide and prepare the food. These customs and the rationale for them can shed considerable light on the later monastic ways of cooking and eating described by Dōgen.

Begging for One's Food

Monks in India (Skt., *bhikshu* and *bhikshuni*, for male and female renunciants) were dependent for food on religious begging (Pali, *pindapatika*, J., *takuhatsu*), a custom that already existed in India before the rise of

Buddhism. According to Brahmanist teaching, the duties of family heads included offering alms of food and clothes to religious practitioners and to people suffering from poverty. A large population of all sorts of religious practitioners was supported in this way.

In Indian Buddhism, a person who vowed to become a monk agreed to follow the monastic regulations called the Vinaya, which is one of the three main divisions, or "baskets," of early Buddhist scriptures. All monks and nuns were supposed to adhere firmly to the numerous rules of the Vinaya throughout their entire lives. In the version of the Vinaya used by the southern Theravada schools, there were two hundred twenty-seven articles for monks, including nearly fifty concerning food; nuns had three hundred eleven articles, including seventy regarding food.

Among these regulations were the Four Essentials, or allowances, fundamental rules governing the necessities of food and drink, clothes, shelter and bedding, and medicine. The first of the Four Essentials declared that monks could only eat food obtained through mendicant practice. In contrast to China and Japan, where rice, wheat, vegetables, and money for clothes were offered as alms, it was the practice in India to place cooked meals directly into the outstretched bowls of monks. Meals prepared in lay households for home use were shared with monks, who were offered their food before the householders themselves ate. In India's hot climate food spoiled quickly, so there was a rule that food prepared in the morning had to be eaten before noon that day.

Monks and nuns were expected to survive primarily by mendicancy, but there were of course some exceptions, and just what was permissible was laid out in detail. Among the exceptions were (1) cases in which all the members of the local sangha were invited to a lay supporter's house for a meal and (2) specific members of the sangha were invited to a lay supporter's house for a meal. In other cases, it seems clear that laypeople brought prepared meals to the monastery, for example: (1) a meal offered by a donor to the entire seasonal community of monks; (2) the drawing of lots for meals when there was not sufficient food for all the members of the sangha; and (3) meals offered to mark special occasions such as the first and the fifteenth day of each month, when the sangha had a ceremony of repentance and renewal of vows (Skt. *uposata*, J. *fusatsu*).

There is no evidence that these early Indian monasteries (*vihara*) had cooking places or utensils. However, particular monks were assigned to taking care of the meals brought to their vihara. The Vinaya lists titles for various roles: monks who distributed offered foods, those who took care of drawing lots, and those who handled different types of food. Names of facilities are also given, such as the food-distributing hall and the eating hall.

Food as Medicine

The fourth essential, medicine, was closely related to food. For one thing, while the category included medicinal items applied externally, such as ointments, most medicines were taken orally. Second, most medicines were made of foodstuffs or closely related products. And third, meals were often considered medicinal to begin with, since their purpose was to maintain physical well-being, not to provide gustatory pleasure.

The fourth essential directed monks to use fermented cow's urine as a medicinal tonic. As with begging, this was in accord with the general customs of India of that era, when the fermented urine of sacred cows was considered an elixir. There were five other medicinal foods—ghee, fermented milk, oil, honey, and sugar—that healthy monks ate during meals and monks who were unwell could eat at any time.

The Vinaya divided medicines into four categories: mealtime medicine, non-mealtime medicine, seven-day medicine, and lifelong medicine. "Mealtime medicine" was actually the regular daily meals, eaten between the early morning and noon. Meals were not usually taken in the afternoon and evening. These regular meals included five kinds of foods: rice, gruel, wheat-flour products, fish, and meat. A few kinds of drinks were permitted, such as rice juice and various milk drinks. These mealtime medicines were recommended for all monks.

"Non-mealtime medicine" included various foods that were "hard," meaning they didn't spoil easily, such as roots, stems, leaves, grasses, fruits, oil, sesame, flour, and brown sugar, which all monks consumed. Healthy monks could eat these during the first part of the day, while those who were unwell were free to eat them at any hour. For those who were ill, regular mealtime foods were also permitted at any time, called in that case "non-mealtime medicines."[4]

"Seven-day medicine" was foods that could withstand spoilage for seven days, and there was a rule against keeping them longer than that. There were five kinds: ghee, oil, honey, sugar, and a variety of fruits and nuts. "Lifelong medicines" could be preserved for a long time, and they could be taken throughout one's life. They were medicines made from dried roots, leaves, fruits, tree saps (resin), and some minerals such as salt.

Early Vinaya texts directed monks to practice mindful contemplation when they received food, clothing, sleeping implements, and to use them with care. Of food the texts say:

> When we receive food offerings we should mindfully contemplate as follows: We do not eat for the sake of our self-satisfaction or to become arrogant. We eat neither to build a sturdy body nor to improve our appearance. We receive food offerings to maintain the body and to repel illness and hunger, to help us practice Buddha's way. Taking this alms food will banish old pains and prevent new pains from springing up. Thus we can sustain a peaceful life.

In short, monks were told to always bear in mind that their meals were simply for the maintenance of their physical body, to assist their practice of the Buddha way. Meals were not occasions for extravagant display, entertainment, or aesthetic pleasure.

The Zen meal verse called the "Five Reflections on Food," chanted at meals in the Sōtō Zen tradition even today, denotes precisely the same idea and sounds like a direct echo of the Vinaya exhortation: "Innumerable labors have brought us this food; we should know how it comes to us. / Receiving this offering, we should reflect on whether our virtue and practice deserve it. / As we desire the natural condition of mind to be free from clinging, we must be free from greed. / We take this meal as medicine to sustain our life. / We receive it for the sake of enlightenment."

Foods meeting the criteria of the Four Essentials had to be not only of certain types but also obtained by mendicant activity. Aside from a few exceptions, any form of obtaining food other than by donation was considered erroneous and was prohibited.

The Vinaya included precise instructions regarding many details of eating in addition to the rules governing begging, what foods and medicines were acceptable, and when they could be eaten. The Vinaya also prescribed the amount of food to eat, defined luxury foods, prohibited alcohol, and defined proper manners for accepting invitations to eat at a donor's house, and for cleaning the food bowl after the meal.

Foods Approved and Disapproved

Fish and meat were acceptable foods for donors to offer and monks to receive and eat. Eating fish and the meat of birds and mammals was quite common from the earliest period of Buddhism through the period of sectarian Buddhism, which began one hundred years after the Buddha's death. Southeast Asian Buddhism inherited that practice and did not prohibit fish and meat in the daily diet of monastics.

The early Mahayana sutras did not mention abstaining from those foods, and most likely the monks and nuns of those periods ate them freely. Chinese and Japanese Mahayana Buddhism began proscribing fish and meat under the influence of the *Nirvana Sutra* and the *Lankavatara Sutra*, which were produced in the Middle Mahayana sutra period (between the second and the fifth centuries). The rationale for abstaining from fish and meat came from the strong emphasis on the idea of compassion in these middle-period Mahayana sutras. The *Lankavatara Sutra* prohibits eating fish and meat primarily because of the idea that the existence of all living beings has been intertwined from the beginning of time, and any living being may have been one's relative in a previous life. To buttress its argument, the sutra offered several other reasons to avoid eating meat: fishmongers and butchers might sell meat adulterated with human flesh, grisly as it might seem; eating meat arouses an atmosphere of impurity, which causes other people to feel fear and prevents monks from feeling compassion; eating meat tarnishes the reputation of the sangha; the uncompassionate mind aroused by meat-eating erases good will; the heavenly beings (*deva*) who are guardians of dharma will eventually abandon meat eaters; meat-eating monks will be liable to have nightmares; wild animals might attack them because of the odor of meat that clings to them. The sutra even goes on to suggest that meat-eating might lead to cannibalism.

For all these reasons, Chinese Buddhism, beginning in the Northern and Southern dynasties period (420–592), strictly prohibited monks from eating meat, as well as from drinking alcohol or using pungent spices. (In Japan, Buddhist priests have been allowed to eat meat since the second half of the nineteenth century, except in some formal training situations.)

Though the monks of the early sangha in India could eat meat, they were prohibited from receiving it under various conditions. Meat was considered tainted and unacceptable, even if it was received as alms, if a monk knew or had reason to believe that the donor had caught and killed an animal in order to offer that meat to the monk. The Vinaya also prohibited particular kinds of meat completely, even if it was not tainted by having been killed especially for a monk. This included the flesh of elephants, horses, dogs, snakes, lions, tigers, leopards, and bears. Outside of these prohibited and tainted types, all meats were to be eaten without discrimination, whenever they were donated, as the appropriate response to the donor's generosity.

The early sutra collection, the *Suttanipata*, included the *Sutra on Tainted Items*, a text that defines "taint." This sutra begins as a defense of Buddhists who eat meat against criticisms by practitioners of other religions. The sutra argues that it is not meat itself but the acts of injuring and killing animals that are tainted. The Buddha called various types of acts besides killing tainted, such as stealing, false speech, and sexual misconduct. Numerous specific acts were also described as tainted, such as the inability to control one's desires, gluttony, nihilistic views, incorrect livelihood, disorderly conduct, betraying friends, being cold-blooded and conceited, and being greedy and ungenerous. But the Buddha nowhere said eating meat was tainted. The sutra goes on to say that unlike meat-eating, superstitious belief and pagan religions and rites are tainted.

Early texts also described erroneous ways of life for monks in terms of four kinds of "incorrect food." Here, too, the error derives not from what the food is but from how it is obtained. The four problematic types were "upward food," "downward food," "centrifugal food," and "centripetal food." "Upward food" is, literally, food obtained by looking up. The *Sutra of the Last Discourse of the Buddha* advised that this meant "looking at the shapes of stars full or on the wane and from them assuming and calculating life," which refers to people make a living by gazing at the stars and moon and counting the days in order to forecast people's fate. That is, it was wrong to accept food in exchange for astrological predictions.

"Downward food" meant food obtained by looking downward. According to the *Last Discourse* this included "all sorts of agricultural activities, cutting wood, plowing the earth," to obtain food. Monks and nuns were forbidden to engage in any agricultural activities or any other manual labor to provide for themselves.

"Centrifugal food" meant food one went out into society to obtain. The *Last Discourse* advised against "participating in social affairs, conveying decrees, appeasing authorities, or engaging in commercial activities." Monks were forbidden to act as couriers for the authorities, to become marriage brokers, to buy and sell goods, or to take any other socially involved role in order to sustain their own life.

Just as monks and nuns were told not to turn outward to society to work for their food, they were also not to turn inward to the occult. Regarding "centripetal food," the *Last Discourse* enjoined against "mixing medicines, acting like a prophet, engaging in sorcery, or creating elixirs for longevity," which meant they were not to engage in divination or sorcery, or to make potions or even medicines for their own gain.

The Merit of Austerity

The most rigorous mendicant monastic life included various prohibitions intended to promote a pure, ascetic practice called *dhuta* practice. There were thirteen of these austerities regulating food, clothing, dwelling, and other matters of daily life, and monks could choose to observe any or all of them. Five of them concerned food: "perpetual begging," "unconditional begging," "just one meal," "just one bowl," and "not eating after mealtime." Let us examine them in turn below.

"To support austerity by begging for food perpetually" meant that a monk who practiced by this rule had to survive solely by mendicant practice throughout his entire life. He was not allowed any of the exceptions to begging spelled out in the Vinaya, such as meals offered to particular monks or to whole groups of monks, and meals offered in honor of special occasions and ceremonies.

The Pali *Annotations of the Vinaya*, additional rules that were formulated later, when Buddhist monastic communal living had been firmly established, added further prohibitions. Practitioners of the dhuta austerity were not allowed to receive meals served when someone arrived as a guest or when someone left, meals intended for monks who were ill and their attendants, local specialties, or special meals marking the change of seasons.

The rule concerning "unconditional begging" addressed a monk's attitudes toward gathering food. When monks went out early in the morning to beg, they were not to attach any conditions to the food they accepted. They were not to choose food based on how rich or poor the donors were, how strong or weak their faith was, or what the quality of the food was. Begging was to be practiced evenly and equally, because mendicancy was not only a means to support monks' lives, it was also a way to teach laypeople the profundity of religious life and to offer them an opportunity to be compassionate. Begging was also supposed to demonstrate selflessness and nonattachment, lack of greed, contentment with life, and the concept of equality. By their attitude and comportment in mendicancy, monks were to help raise laypeople's religious consciousness.

"Just one meal," the austere rule of begging only enough for a single meal, is literally "begging food at one sitting." When a monk received a meal, he was to eat it then. He could neither save some to eat another time, nor leave the meal and return to it later. Similarly, the fourth austerity, the rule of "taking only one bowl of food" meant a monk ate one bowlful and no more, and received all his food mixed together in the same bowl.

"Not eating after mealtime" is a reiteration of the normal Vinaya rule against eating after noon. Its inclusion in the *dhuta*, or austerity rules, perhaps shows how difficult it was to follow.

These austere rules were intended to help monks cultivate nonattachment, lack of greed, satisfaction with less, less illness, and less suffering. Furthermore, the Vinaya stated, this living example of restraint would lead laypeople to pay homage to the buddha dharma, and it would lead people to awareness and compassion.

There is a story about Shakyamuni Buddha visiting his native land several years after he had attained enlightenment that illustrates the religious foundation of begging. The Buddha's father, the ruler of the Shakya people, welcomed his son's visit and offered a feast in his honor. The next morning the Buddha visited each and every house in the area, begging. The king thought his son was going about merely to obtain food. He told the Buddha that it embarrassed him, and asked him to stop immediately. The king found begging at each house incomprehensible, and he feared that people might think he was not feeding his son. The Buddha said, "I am begging because this was taught by my ancestors." The king replied, "Among all my ancestors, since the first Indian king, no one has done any begging." The Buddha replied, "The ancestors I meant were my predecessors in the buddha dharma. Since Dipankara Buddha, all buddhas have upheld the right form of life by religious begging." For Shakyamuni, mendicancy was a pure religious act that went far beyond the fulfillment of bodily needs.

Brahmans were the upper class in Indian society at that time and they, too, considered begging lowly behavior. Early Buddhist literature relates an incident in which Shakyamuni Buddha had an exchange with some brahmans and, as a concluding note, presented them with a religious verse, a *gatha*. The brahmans were highly impressed with it and offered the Buddha a generous meal as a token of their gratitude. Shakyamuni said in response that he could not accept the food as payment for his teaching. For Shakyamuni, receiving food in exchange for an act of any kind was a form of possessiveness; begging for food ought to be nonpossessive, nonattached, and nondiscriminating, and furthermore, it must always be unconditional. Many brahmans did not comprehend this and scornfully thought mendicant monks were mere beggars. Many religious renunciants (*sannyasin*) at this time recited gathas in exchange for food, and the brahmans had thought that Buddhists were no exception.

In this early period, it was thought that both monks who practiced mendicancy and lay people who offered food as alms received great merit. In the later period of sectarian Buddhism, a few centuries after Buddha's death, at the time of King Ashoka, the situation began to change. Buddhist monasteries and temples started to receive large donations of goods and land, and became prosperous. This wealth was sufficient to maintain them, and monks no longer needed to beg. As a result, contacts between monks and laypeople became less frequent and the monks' teaching activities declined. It was partly in consequence of this that Buddhism gradually waned as a religion of the common people in India.

Enlightened Life in the Mahayana

The rules governing monastic life changed considerably between the Vinaya of the early centuries of Buddhism in India and the rules for Zen monks of later Mahayana eras in China and Japan. Chinese Chan and Japanese Zen monasteries' "pure rules" (Ch., *qinggui*, J., *shingi*) were developed to regulate life in very different circumstances and based on very different underlying assumptions.

The differences between their basic viewpoints are significant. The Vinaya's purpose was to guide and regulate those who were not yet enlightened. Beginning in the early years after Shakyamuni, it was thought that if one lived according to the Vinaya and attained enlightenment and became a sage, even at a low level, one's practice of the Vinaya would be firmly established, and one's views of the world and life clarified as well. This was the stage of self-constraint, which led to neither going astray nor committing any evil deeds, even if tempted by others; neither would one be at any further risk of losing one's belief and defecting to other religions. There was thus no further need for rules of conduct after enlightenment was attained.

According to legend, in the eleven years following the Buddha's enlightenment, his disciples all reached the level of *arhat*, the condition of being free from all craving and defilement and of possessing perfect knowledge. Thus, no one did anything wrong and there was no need for rules during this time. But once the Buddhist sangha grew larger there were Buddhist monks who acted wrongly, and rules were created case by case until finally the number of rules reached into the hundreds. The rules were considered essential to the monks' and nuns' progress.

Before his death Shakyamuni said to his close disciple and attendant Ananda, "After my death, minor rules of the Vinaya can be discarded." However, the meaning of "minor rules" was unclear and so all the rules were preserved. If the Buddhist sangha had continued to be made up only of people of the caliber of Shakyamuni and his enlightened disciples, the rules would not have been needed or created, but in point of fact, the rules were supremely important for monks who had not yet attained enlightenment in the centuries prior to the emergence of the Mahayana movement.

Mahayana Buddhism, on the other hand, taught a return to the ultimate truth taught by Shakyamuni Buddha. According to Mahayana teachings people are not different from buddhas, so human practice and enlightenment cannot be different from the practice and enlightenment of buddhas. Zen Buddhism has sometimes been called Tathagata Zen, or Ancestral-teacher Zen, because it puts special emphasis on this ultimate truth (J., *shōtai dai-ichigi*, literally "the first principle of the Buddha's holy teaching").

Dōgen espoused and taught the oneness of practice and enlightenment. The core of his teaching was that true enlightenment exists inherently in practice and that daily practice should be in exact accord with that unity. The spirit of Dōgen's *Rules of Purity for Eiheiji* was that the concrete day-to-day activities in Zen monasteries were nothing other than buddhas' practice.

Where the Vinaya was a blueprint showing unenlightened monks how to develop into enlightened arhats or buddhas, Mahayana rules like the shingi were guidelines for buddhas to learn to express their nature clearly. The Vinaya was a system of external controls the individual was called on to accept, whereas Mahayana rules were based on the monk's or nun's autonomy and self-governance.

A second, related difference is that in the extensive, formal, and specific rules of the Vinaya, the separation between monks and lay believers was very strict. Monks had to follow a course of right livelihood centered on mendicant practice and aiming at the purity of arhatship. Laypeople could not elevate themselves to the level of arhat, although their lives, too, were regulated by the law of cause and effect. The goal of their lives was to exert effort in their work. They could hope that their good deeds in this lifetime would lead to their being reborn into a life in which they could be ordained, practice the buddha dharma in the form of the Vinaya, and perhaps become an arhat.

In Mahayana Buddhism, on the other hand, there is no fundamental separation between monks and laypeople. A layperson could practice selfless giving (*dana*) and uphold the lay precepts. Although tied to this mundane world, the laity could also experience the truth of the supermundane world.

In Zen monasteries, everyday life is considered the very life of the Buddha if things are done with way-seeking mind. Carrying water, gathering firewood, and preparing meals for other monks are all sacred practices of the ultimate truth. For both ordained and laypeople, work in daily life is seen as the same as practicing the way through zazen.

For Zen Buddhists, the often-quoted saying "Everyday mind is the way" has been a style of life. As *Instructions for the Cook* states, we can build a buddha's jeweled temple with one blade of grass, and we can enter into a speck of dust to turn the great dharma wheel. This is a spirit very different from the regulations in the Vinaya. In essence, in the Mahayana it is essential for each of us to consider ourself a bodhisattva, to stand on the ground of awakening, and to maintain the constantly awakening and striving mind. Then the intent, the act, and the effect of our action will all accord harmoniously with the way.

Rules for Meals in China

Hisao Shinohara

C odes governing conduct emerge quite naturally in developing communities of all sorts, often following a common pattern. People gather informally around a leader, perhaps a religious master possessing unusual ability, and as the number of followers grows, a community begins to form. Soon a system is needed for the orderly function of the group, and the leaders are likely to turn to earlier models for guidance as they craft new systems. Buddhism is of course no exception to this kind of evolutionary pattern and has repeatedly created new rules based in part on existing ones.

Dōgen wrote *Instructions for the Cook* at the age of thirty-eight, ten years after he returned from China and four years after he founded Kōshō Hōrinji monastery. There is no record that he ever served as tenzo in China, but the practices relating to cooking at the monasteries he visited there, which were guided by the "rules of purity for Chan monasteries" (Ch. *qinggui*; J. *shingi*), made a tremendous impact on him. Dōgen was interested in all matters of the monastic institution, and he was especially impressed with the monastic rules attributed to Baizhang (720–814), which he recommended to his students, saying, "Students of Zen must obey the *Rules of Baizhang* diligently. Those rules govern the ceremonies of ordination, adherence to the precepts, zazen [sitting practice], and so forth."[1]

Whether Dōgen actually read Baizhang's monastic rules is unclear, but his reverence for the ancient rules was lifelong.[2] Dōgen may not have been able to consult any specific text of Baizhang's rules when he wrote *Rules of Purity for Eiheiji*, but he definitely had access to one of the earliest of the monastic rules transmitted to Japan, the *Chanyuan Qinggui* (*Rules of Purity for the Chan Monastery*), which was compiled in 1103. Two other Chan monastic rules were codified in China in the following century and were later transmitted to Japan, the *Ruzhong Riyong Qinggui* (*Rules of Purity for Entering the Community and Daily Functions*), dating to 1209, and the slightly later *Conglin Jiaoding Qinggui Zongyao* (*Essentials of the Revised Rules of Purity for Public Monasteries*).³

Dōgen not only read the *Chanyuan Qinggui* but also turned to it as a resource for his own monastic rule. This passage in *Instructions for the Cook*, for instance, is drawn from the Chinese pure rule: "One should maintain a way-seeking mind, make adjustments in accord with the occasion, and see to it that the great assembly receives what is necessary and is at ease."

The great number of passages in *Instructions for the Cook* that utilize the *Chanyuan Qinggui* demonstrate how important a source the Chinese text was for Dōgen. *Instructions for the Cook* is virtually modeled on the much shorter section on the responsibilities of the cook in the Chinese text. The compiler of the *Chanyuan Qinggui*, Zongze, does not explicitly discuss the tenzo's attitude, which is so central to Dōgen's rule, and he only describes the gist of the tenzo's responsibilities, but he lays these out clearly in a way that points to the underlying ethos. For example, Zongze specified: "The tenzo, who is in charge of the work at the kitchen, also eats there, but his food must be exactly the same as that of the other monks."

Even a monk responsible for cooking in the monastery was not set apart from the other monks and did not have any special benefits. The spirit of equality was of the utmost importance in monastic life, but equality is easily forgotten, so it was necessary to mention it repeatedly. When Dōgen was at Kenninji after his return from China, he saw that the tenzo there was so in name only—that is, he did not fulfill the duties of his role himself but assigned them to others, which undercut the spirit of Zongze's teaching.

The *Chanyuan Qinggui* addresses the tenzo's attitude through his actions again when the meal is being served: "When the midday meal or morning gruel has been properly prepared and placed on the table, the cook dons his kesa, spreads his sitting cloth, faces the sangha hall [where the monks eat], burns incense, and makes nine prostrations." Dōgen inherited this tradition, including that the tenzo is to prepare meals using the same dedication to religious practice as is maintained by those meditating in the monks' hall.

The *Ruzhong Riyong Qinggui*, the earlier of the thirteenth-century rules, is thought to have been written for novices. Given its date of publication and its use in Song-dynasty China, Dōgen may have consulted it during his time in China. There is no decisive evidence of this in his *Instructions for the Cook*, but there are similarities in the underlying attitudes of carefulness, harmonizing with the group, and concern for one's neighbors. Here is a passage from the *Ruzhong Riyong Qinggui*:

> When you eat, the food should be brought to your mouth, never your mouth to the food. While you are handling your eating implements, as when holding the bowl or spoon in your hands or placing it on the table, never talk. You must neither cough nor sniffle. If you have to sneeze, cover your nose with the sleeve of your robe. You must not scratch your head, so dandruff will not fall into the bowl of the person next to you.
>
> When you eat rice or soup, do not make any noise. When you are waiting for the food, close your mouth. When you eat rice, neither dig it out from the center of the bowl nor make a big ball out of it. Be careful not to drop your rice. You must not eat even one kernel of rice with your hand.
>
> You must not send a breeze over the next person when you fan yourself. You must neither place wet food in your main bowl, nor pour soup into it and eat rice mixed with the soup. Do not dig out food from the vegetable bowl to mix with rice in your main bowl when you eat.
>
> When you eat your meals, watch the monks in the upper and lower sides of the hall and do not be later than the others. Never clean your bowls before the second serving ends. Do not suck the bowl-cleaning stick or make noise.

When the specific regulations regarding eating meals in the various written texts are compared, it is clear that the spirit of the early twelfth-century *Chanyuan Qinggui* is reflected in the early thirteenth-century *Ruzhong Riyong Qinggui* and in the slightly later *Ruzhong Xuzhi* of 1263, as it also is in Dōgen's *Instructions for the Cook*.[4] It does not take a great stretch of the imagination to see in all of them deep traces of the ancient tradition known at least apocryphally as Baizhang's "old rules of purity."

Ancient Chinese Meal Guidelines

The Chan monastic rules that Dōgen turned to for his *Instructions for the Cook* built in turn on a long history of attention in China to cooking and eating. The Confucian classics known as the Four Books and the Five Classics, which were written a thousand years or more before the Chan rules of purity, give abundant evidence of this focus.[5] These nine classical texts were the golden rules of the Chinese intellectual tradition, teaching self-cultivation to many generations of educated Chinese. The *Analects*, one of the Four Books, records dialogues between Confucius (551–479 BCE) and his students and lays out the master's eating habits in detail, offering a model for his followers to emulate:

> During purification for the sacrifice he changed what he ate and where he sat. Polished rice was fine, and minced meat. He didn't eat sour rice or rancid fish or spoiled meat. He didn't eat anything that looked or smelled bad. He didn't eat food that wasn't well cooked and in season, or food that wasn't properly sauced. Even when there was plenty of meat, he only ate enough to balance the ch'i of the rice. Only in wine did he set no limits, but he never drank himself into confusion. He wouldn't drink wine from a wine shop or eat meat from a market. And though he didn't refuse ginger, he ate it only sparingly.
>
> After the state sacrifice he never kept the meat overnight. And he never kept meat more than three days after the family sacrifice. After three days, he wouldn't eat it.
>
> He didn't speak at meals, and he didn't talk in bed. He made an offering of even the simplest rice and vegetable, broth and melon—and he did so with the greatest solemnity.[6]

Some issues mentioned here seem to be perennial: avoiding spoiled foods, being particular about the sources of food, balancing foods, not overindulging, and solemnizing eating with ritual. Modern annotations to this text describe the ritual of food offerings made during the meal, saying that it consisted of a small amount of rice placed on the utensil to pay respect to the ancients who created food and cuisine. This ancient custom is surprisingly similar to the daily meal offering in Zen Buddhist meals, in which each person puts a small morsel of rice aside on the tip of one of their utensils (a stick for cleaning the last bits of food from one's eating bowls), as an offering for wandering hungry ghosts (*preta*). The specific object of the food offering is somewhat different, but the underlying attitude of respectful symbolic offering to invisible spirits is similar.

The *Book of Rites* (*Liji*), one of the Four Books, gives detailed instructions on serving food, indicating how even the most mundane aspects of eating are important enough to ritualize:

> Generally speaking, the rituals of offering food to someone who is important must be as follows. Meat with bones must be placed at the left side of the table, raw sliced meat on the right side. Rice is set in front of the guest on the left. Soup must be at the right side. . . .
>
> The host must consider the comfort and convenience of the guest. Even if the social position of the guest is lower than that of the host, the host comes before him to offer the food. The guest takes his food and goes to the lower section of the hall to eat his meal, but the host tells his guest not to take the lower seat. The host then leaves his seat to perform the rite of revering the patriarch of food. In the ceremony the host offers different dishes of food [at the shrine], one by one in proper order.[7]

This description of general table manners shows the ancients making mealtime food offerings to the ancestors in the midst of their meals, again, not unlike the Zen custom. The host paid his respects to the patriarch of food during the meal as well as at the outset, ceremonially taking a small portion of food and placing it between the food stands. This, too, resembles the Zen meal offering. The *Book of Rites* continues with instructions on manners for guest and host that reveal their underlying intent:

> When you eat soup or rice from a container shared among everyone at the table, you must not eat until you are satiated. You must [always] reserve some food for others. . . .
>
> Do not make rice into balls to eat. That would make it appear that you wish to eat a lot, and this is improper. If the rice sticks to your hand, do not detach and return it to the container. Others may think it is not clean. Do not eat soup with an open mouth and do not sip it with a loud noise. It

would look as though you despise the food. Do not chew the bones. One might think that you do not have refined manners. Chewing bones might also suggest that you are starved. Don't take a large amount of food. One might think you are greedy. . . .

When you sip the soup, the solid stuff in the soup must not be swallowed without chewing. In these actions, too, you might look as though you were in a hurry. Do not add any seasonings [at the table]. It would look as though you are unsatisfied with the taste. Food pickled in brine must not be sipped. One might think you are complaining about the taste and also implying that the taste was not salty enough. If a guest sips the brine, the host will apologize to save the guest's pride, saying there was not enough salt. . . . When one receives fruit with pits, one must place the pits inside one's garments, so as not to give the appearance of discarding something one has been given.

These Confucian texts address attitudes and rituals of eating that long antedate Zen monastic rules. Zen, or Chan, built on the spiritual history of China and on the adaptations Buddhism made to fit into Chinese society. It crystallized a very long tradition of Chinese wisdom.

One example of this is the Zen teaching method of bringing out students' innate abilities rather than imposing something external on them. Confucius mentioned the concept of *ren*, or "humanity," seventy times in his *Analects*, personalizing it to each student's ability rather than suggesting a uniform teaching for all. According to the *Analects*, the master said: "I never instruct those who aren't full of passion, and I never enlighten those who aren't struggling to explain themselves. If I show you one corner and you can't show me the other three, I'll say nothing more."[8] Confucius did not teach unless his students had studied by themselves, making great efforts to get through their difficulties, and had reached a stage close to the master's expectations for them. His teaching made no room for the spoon-feeding that is so common in modern education, in which teachers lay everything out from the beginning in detail for their students.

I think we can find right here the origin of the education methods of Zen masters, which have been likened to the simultaneous pecking from inside a shell of a chick ready to break through and the pecking from outside by the hen trying to free the chick.

Dōgen's Instructions for the Cook

Instructions for the Cook records Dōgen's own study and practice. It shows his frustration at not being able to find true practice in Japanese monasteries and his satisfaction at completing true practice in China. It candidly describes his mental struggles and his earnest efforts to understand the monastic rules he encountered there. Since this book was written a relatively short time after his return from China, his images of Chinese monasteries and his encounters with Chinese masters and the old tenzo at Mount Ashoka Monastery are vivid. Dōgen always taught Buddhism using concrete examples, and in *Instructions for the Cook* he used a lively question-and-answer style, as seen in his conversations with the old tenzo. Also, Dōgen wrote in the vernacular language of daily speech, which suggests that he recorded the dialogue as it happened. If Dōgen had converted his writings into a more literary style, or if he had not used the question-and-answer format, the vividness of the scenes he described would have been lost.

Dōgen taught not only zazen, but the Zen practice of daily life, and he taught with particular care the way we should eat. At this early stage in his life, when *Instructions for the Cook* was written, he was establishing the style of teaching that would become his hallmark. Dōgen contradicted the view common in Japan in his time that cooking duties in the monastery were inferior activities. He equated the tenzo's duty with the fully legitimate practice of Buddhism and rejected the concept of superior and inferior tasks. This message is relevant even to the lives of busy householders today. *Instructions for the Cook* can guide everyone, lay and ordained, to see just how profound their everyday activities really are. Quite apart from questions of formal spiritual practice, people can concern themselves with food preparation this one day, this one time, and thus transform their efforts into the undertaking of the path. Dōgen wrote that the work of the tenzo was identical to the accomplishment of the way of the Buddha, and his *Instructions for the Cook* teaches the spirit of a life of Zen through its examination of the role of the tenzo as a way to express wholehearted and magnanimous life.

■ ■ ■

1   Dōgen, *Shōbōgenzō Zuimonki*, 1-2.
2   As Griffith Foulk said in the notes to the text translation, modern scholars think Baizhang's rules did not exist. There may never have been a codified

set of rules by Baizhang. What there was, in Dōgen's time, was a central principle that was attributed to the very famous and revered Baizhang, that a day of not working was a day of not eating. Dōgen, like the Chinese masters he encountered, thought Baizhang was literally the first Zen master to establish a Zen monastery and a set of rules of purity (shingi).

3   See the translation by Yifa, "The Rules of Purity for the Chan Monastery: An annotated translation of the *Chanyuan qinggui*," Ph.D. dissertation, Yale University, 1996. The second two texts, which were compiled in 1209 and 1293, respectively, have not yet been analyzed or translated into English.
4   *Ruzhung Xuzhi* was a simplified rules of purity as an instruction for novice monks.
5   The Four Books are the *Great Learning*, *Doctrine of the Mean*, *Analects*, and *Mencius*. The Five Classics are the *Books of Songs*, *History*, *Changes*, and *Rites*, and the *Spring and Autumn Annals*. Shinohara notes his omission of any discussion of Daoist food practices due to limitations of space.
6   This is from the "Xiangdang" (Village Folks) section of the *Analects*. Shinohara used a modern Japanese translation of the Books and Classics. Rather than retranslate these in a third-hand way, the editors have used the modern translation into English directly from the Chinese by David Hinton (*The Analects*, Counterpoint, 1998); here, pp. 105–6.
7   This is from the "Dianli" (Manners) section of the *Book of Rites* (*Liji*).
8   This is from the "Shuer" (Commentary) section of the *Analects* (Hinton, p. 68).

Appendices

Glossary

abbot's quarters (J. *hōjō*, 方丈): Hōjō literally means a room of one square *jō* (in ancient China one *jō* was 225 cm, about 7 feet; in Japan one *jō* is 303 cm, about 10 feet). This name originally came from the *Vimalakirti-nirdesa Sutra*. Although Vimalakirti stayed in a one-square-*jō* room, myriads of beings were able to occupy the space with him at the same time.

administrator (J. *chiji*, 知事): According to the *Rules of Purity for Chan Monasteries* there were four administrators (or stewards) to take care of temple affairs in monasteries. These were the *kan'in* (comptroller), *ino* (monks' supervisor, or rector), *tenzo* (cook), and *shissui* (work leader). Later in Song China, the functions of the *kan'in* were divided into three; the *tsūsu* (prior, or overseer), the *kansu* (comptroller) and the *fūsu* (assistant competroller or treasurer), so there were these six administrators, or stewards.

all-consuming (single color) engagement of the way (J. *isshiki no bendo*, 一色の弁道): *Isshiki* literally means single color; this term means wholehearted, undivided, pure practice. In this book, we translate this expression in various ways, such as single color practice, all-consuming unvarying engagement of the way, single color of diligently engaging in the way, and engaging the way.

Analects (J. *Rongo*, 論語): The collection of the sayings of Confucius. One of the most important classics in Confucianism.

ancestral teacher (J. *soshi*, 祖師): In Chinese Zen (Chan), masters who had transmitted the dharma from Shakyamuni Buddha were called ancestral (patriarchal) teachers.

Ancestral Teacher Zen (J. *soshizen*, 祖師禅): The Southern Zen School was called by this name because it was transmitted by the first patriarch (ancestor) Bodhidharma from India.

Ashoka (Ch. Ayuwang, J. Aikuō, 阿育王): King Ashoka (d. ca. 232 BCE) was a warrior king who unified India and then became a devout patron of Buddhism, building many temples. He is considered the model of an awakened Buddhist political leader. In China, there was a monastery built on a mountain named after King Ashoka near the place where Dōgen practiced. It received this name in the year 281 when a monk found an old *stupa* on the mountain and thought that the stupa was one of the eighty-four thousand stupas built by King Ashoka to enshrine the Buddha's relics. Later the monastery named Ayuwang temple (J. Aikuōji, King Ashoka Temple) was established on this mountain.

assistant comptroller (J. *fūsu*, 副寺): One of the six administrators (or stewards) in the Zen monastery. The fūsu was in charge of financial affairs, much like a treasurer.

Avalokiteshvara Bodhisattva (J. *kannon*, 観音): Avalokiteshvara is one of the ideal bodhisattvas in Mahayana Buddhism. Avalokiteshvara is a symbol of Buddha's compassion.

begging rounds (Skt. *pindapata*, J. *takuhatsu*, 托鉢): Takuhatsu, literally "to entrust or hold up a bowl," is ritualized begging done by Buddhist monks. Monks hold the bowl at nose height with the thumb and first two fingers of both hands when they go out soliciting donations, usually food and money. In Japan all monks in training go out on alms rounds, and some priests continue the practice later on as well.

Bendōwa (弁道話): Talk on Wholehearted Practice of the Way. Dōgen wrote Bendōwa in 1231, before he established his first monastery, Kōshōji.

bodhisattva (J. *bosatsu*, 菩薩): Mahayana Buddhists called themselves bodhisattvas, as this was also the title used for Shakyamuni Buddha before he attained buddhahood. A bodhisattva is a person who has aroused *bodhi-citta* (awakening mind).

Book of Rites (Ch. *Liji*, J. *Raiki*, 礼記): One of the five important scriptures in Confucianism.

brahman: One of the four classes in the Indian caste system. The brahmans had religious authority.

buddhas and ancestors (J. *busso*, 仏祖): The people who have transmitted the buddha dharma to the next generation through history.

buddha dharma (J. *buppō*, 仏法): Buddha dharma refers to the Buddha's teachings or the truth the Buddha taught.

buddha's children (J. *busshi*, 仏子): In China, Buddhists were considered to be in Buddha's family and each Buddhist practitioner was Buddha's child. Buddha's child also refers to the bodhisattvas who have aroused bodhi-mind and aim to become buddhas in the future.

buddha eye (J. *butsugen*, 仏眼): The buddha eye is a symbol of Buddha's perfect wisdom, which penetrates everything. It is one of the five eyes.

The other four being: the physical eye (肉眼); the divine eye (天眼), the eye of heavenly beings, which can see very far even in darkness; the wisdom eye (慧眼), the eye that sees the reality of interdependent origination; and the dharma eye (法眼), which sees with a compassionate heart as well as with wisdom.

buddha hall (J. *butsuden*, 仏殿): One of the seven major buildings in a Zen monastery.

buddha land (J. *hōōsetsu*, 宝殿刹): *Setsudo* (刹土) is the transliteration of the Skanskrit word *kshetra*, which means the land. According to the *Zengaku Daijiten*, *setsu* (刹) refers to the center pole of a pagoda or a pole set in front of the Buddha hall, so that *hōōsetsu* may refer to Buddhist temples.

buddha mind (J. *busshin*, 仏心): Buddha's great compassionate mind.

buddha nature (仏性): *Buddhata* or *buddhatva* in Sanskrit. In the Mahayana teaching buddha nature is considered to be the capacity, inherent in all sentient beings, for becoming a buddha. Dōgen said that one's whole being is buddha nature (*Shōbōgenzō* "Buddha Nature").

buddha's light (J. *butsukōmyō*, 仏光明): A symbol of buddha's wisdom and compassion.

buddha way (J. *butsudō*, 仏道): The path that leads practitioners to buddhahood. In China, *Dao* (way) was also used as a translation of the Sanskrit word *bodhi* (awakening). So, buddha way can also refer to Buddha's (or to a buddha's) awakening.

buddha work (J. *butsuji*, 仏事): Activities that expound and exalt the buddha dharma. In modern Japan, Buddhist ceremonies such as funeral services and memorial services for lay believers are called *butsuji*.

common quarters (J. *shuryō*, 衆寮): The *shuryō* is one of the seven major buildings in the Zen monastery, where monks can relax, read, and have tea. Avalokiteshvara is enshrined at the center of this building.

comptroller (J. *kansu*, 監寺): One of the six temple administrators or stewards. The comptroller is the assistant of the prior or overseer (*tsūsu*).

Compendious Nirvana Sutra (J. *Butsuyuikyōgyō*, 仏遺教経): *The Sutra of the Last Discourse of the Buddha*.

cook (J. *tenzo*, 典座): The *tenzo* (cook) is one of the six administrators (stewards) in the Zen monastery and is in charge of the preparation of meals.

dana (J. *fuse*, 布施): *Dana* (offering, or generosity) is one of the six perfections (*paramitas*) in Mahayana Buddhism. For example, monks can offer dharma teachings, and lay people can offer food and other necessities to monks.

demigods (Skt. *asura*, J. *ashura*, 阿修羅): Asuras occupy one of the six realms of *samsara*. This is also translated as the realm of the fighting spirits.

dharma (J. *hō*, 法): Dharma can have many meanings, such as beings, Buddha's teaching, the truth Buddha taught, natural law, method, and moral code.

The Dharma for Taking Food (J. *Fushuku Hanpō*, 赴粥飯法): One of the six independent articles in Dōgen's *Rules of Purity for Eiheiji*, in which Dōgen prescribed the manner of taking meals using *ōryōki* bowls in the monks' hall.

dharma wheel (J. *hōrin*, 法輪, Skt. *dharmacakra*): The dharma wheel refers to the Buddha's teaching.

dhuta (J. *zuda*, 頭陀): A set of twelve or thirteen points of practice for Buddhist monks, including rules for eating food obtained by begging, living outside, and practicing begging without discrimination among rich and poor families.

dhyana (J. *zen*, Ch. *chan*, 禅): The Sanskrit word for meditation.

Dipankara Buddha (J. *Nentōbutsu*, 燃燈仏): One of the buddhas of the past, from whom Shakyamuni Buddha first received the prediction that he would attain buddhahood in the future.

Eiheiji (永平寺): Eiheiji (Eternal Peace Monastery) is the monastery founded by Dōgen in 1244 in Echizen (present-day Fukui Prefecture). Today Eiheiji is one of the two major monasteries of the Japanese Sōtō school.

Eihei Kōroku (永平広録): The *Eihei Kōroku* is the collection of Dōgen's formal discourses (*jōdō*) in the dharma hall.

elder's mind (J. *rōshin*, 老心); also translated as nurturing mind, or parental mind: One of the three inner attitudes the *tenzo* and other monks at Zen monasteries should maintain.

engaging the way (J. *bendō*, 弁道): Wholeheartedly engaging the way. This expression is used in the title of *Bendōhō*, the second section of *Rules of Purity for Eiheiji*, and in *Bendōwa* written in 1331.

Five Reflections on Food (J. *Gokan no Ge*, 五観の偈): A verse chanted by monks in Zen monasteries at meals. Dōgen quotes this verse in the *Dharma for Taking Food*.

Fukanzazengi (Universal Recommendation of Zazen, 普勧坐禅儀): *Fukanzazengi* is the manual of zazen practice that Dōgen wrote right after returning from China in 1227.

Flower Garland Sutra (Skt. *Mahavaipulya-buddhavatamsaka-sutra*, J. *Kegon-kyō* 華厳経): One of the most important sutras in early Mahayana Buddhism.

gasshō (合掌): A traditional Buddhist gesture, often a greeting, with palms joined together in front of one's face, with fingers straight up and fingertips about at nose level, hands one width away from the face. Bowing in gassho shows gratitude and respect.

gatha: Gatha is a Sanskrit word for a verse or poem used in the sutras.

grandmotherly heart (J. *rōbashin*, 老婆心): A compassionate heart like a grandmother's for her grandchildren.

great assembly (J. *daishu*, 大衆): The monks at Zen monasteries are called the great assembly.

great mind (J. *daishin*, 大心) or magnanimous mind: One of the three mental attitudes practitioners at Zen monasteries should maintain, the other two being joyful mind and nurturing mind.

hall manager (J. *dōsu*, 堂司): Another name for the *ino* (monks' supervisor).

Heart Sutra (J. *Hannya Shingyō*, 般若心経): Skt. *Maha-prajnaparamita-hridaya-sutra*. One of the most important and popular Mahayana sutras. In it Avalokiteshvara proclaims the teaching of *prajna paramita*, or emptiness.

Hinayana (J. *shōjō*, 小乗): This word literally means smaller vehicle and was used by Mahayana Buddhists to indicate Sectarian Buddhism before the Mahayana.

joyful mind (J. *kishin*, 喜心): One of the three mental attitudes that all practitioners at Zen monasteries should maintain.

jisha (侍者): The personal attendant of the abbot of a monastery.

Kennin Monastery (建仁寺): Kenninji was the first Zen monastery in Japan and was founded by Eisai, who introduced Rinzai Zen from China. Dōgen practiced with Eisai's disciple Myōzen at Kenninji for seven years before he went to China. He also lived there for three years after returning to Japan.

kitchen god (J. *sōkō* 竃公): Literally, the spirit who protects the fire in the stove. The *tenzo* or *tenzo*'s attendant chants the *Daihishin-dharani* in front of this god in the kitchen in Sōtō monasteries.

kōan (公案): A story or dialogue about former masters that is used as an object of meditation or study.

labor administrator (J. *shissui*, 直歳): One of the six administrators in the Zen monastery. The *shissui* is in charge of work (*samu*), including the maintenance of temple buildings and other temple property, overseeing lay workers, etc.

Lankavatara Sutra (Skt. *Lankavatara-sutra*, J. *Ryogakyō*, 楞伽経): One of the Mahayana sutras valued in early Chinese Zen. This sutra teaches the idea of three worlds that are only mind.

Lotus Sutra (Skt. *Saddharmapundarika-sutra*, J. *Myōhō-renge-kyō*, 妙法蓮華経): One of the most important Mahayana sutras, emphasizing *eka-yana* (one vehicle) teaching.

Mahayana Buddhism (J. *Daijō Bukkyō*, 大乗仏教): Mahayana literally means great vehicle. It is also called the Bodhisattva-yana or Buddha-yana. This expression was used by Mahayana Buddhists to make a distinction between their ultimate goal and that of *hinayana* or *shravaka-yana* (the vehicle of self-emancipation). The Mahayana stresses the salvation of all beings. Mahayana Buddhism was transmitted to Japan through China and Korea.

Manjushri (J. *Monjushiri*, 文殊師利): One of the ideal bodhisattvas in Mahayana Buddhism. The embodiment of Buddha's wisdom, Manjushri is enshrined at the center of the monks' hall in Zen monasteries.

Model for Engaging the Way (J. *Bendōhō*) (弁道法): *Bendōhō* is one of the six sections in the *Rules of Purity for Eiheiji*, in which Dōgen prescribes the manner of practice in the monks' hall.

monks' hall (J. *sōdō* 僧堂): One of the seven major buildings in Zen monasteries. The resident monks sleep, practice zazen, and eat meals in the monks' hall. Manjushri is enshrined at the center of the hall.

monks' supervisor (J. *ino*, 維那): The supervisor or rector of the monk's hall, and of the monks' conduct in general; one of the six temple administrators.

Mount Sumeru (J. *shumisen*, 須弥山): The mountain at the center of the cosmos, in ancient Indian cosmology. In Zen temples, the main altar in the buddha hall is called the *shumi-dan*.

Nirvana Sutra (Skt. *Maha-parinirvana-sutra* 涅槃経): One of the Mahayana sutras. The theory of buddha nature appears in this sutra.

Nurturing mind (J. *rōshin*, 老心); also, elder's mind, parental mind: One of the three inner attitudes the *tenzo* and other monks at Zen monasteries should maintain.

ōryōki (応量器): A set of five eating bowls with a wrapping cloth, wiping cloth, lap cloth, utensil bag with utensils, and lacquered paper place mat. The word *ōryōki* is used both for the whole set and for just the largest bowl.

practice period (J. *ango*, 安居): The monastic practice period was held in the rainy season in India for ninety days. Japanese Zen monasteries have two practice periods each year, in the summer and in the winter.

postulant (J. *anja* 行者): A personal attendant of monks in important positions. In Song China this position was filled by lay trainees, but these days in a Japanese Sōtō monastery it is held by junior monks.

prefects (J. *chōshu*, 頭首): The six heads of the different monastic departments are all known as prefects. They are the head monk (*shuso*), the head scribe or secretary (*shoki*), the librarian (*zōsu*), the guest manager (*shika*), the bath attendant (*yokusu*), and the buddha-hall manager (*chiden*).

prior (J. *tsūsu*, 都寺): The overseer or general director of a monastery, one of the six temple administrators.

reverend preceptor (J. *oshō*, 和尚): The Chinese transliteration of the Sanskrit word *upadhaya*. In Indian Buddhism, the *upadhaya* is the main teacher when a monk was ordained. They also needed two teachers called *acaryas* for the ordination ceremony as witnesses.

rōshi (老師): Rōshi is a title for an old and respected teacher.

Rules of Purity for Chan Monasteries (Ch. *Chanyuan Qinggui*, J. *Zen'en Shingi*, 禅苑清規): The *Zen'en Shingi* of 1103 is the oldest rule for Zen monastic practice now known.

Rules of Purity for Eiheiji (J. *Eihei Shingi* 永平清規): *Rules of Purity for Eiheiji* is a collection of six independent articles Dōgen wrote regarding the rules for monastic practice at Eiheiji. Later, it was compiled and published as the text *Eihei Shingi*.

Rules of Purity for Temple Administrators (J. *Chiji Shingi*, 知事清規): One of the six sections of the *Rules of Purity for Eiheiji*, in which Dōgen collected many examples of Chinese Zen masters who practiced as administrators.

sangha (J. *sōgya*, 僧伽): Sangha is one of the three treasures, or jewels in Buddhism; it is the community of people who practice Buddha's teachings.

Sectarian Buddhism (J. *buha bukkyō*, 部派仏教): Sectarian Buddhism refers to the Buddhist communities and their teachings after the original sangha was split into Theravada and Mahasangika sects, before Mahayana Buddhism was established. These original two sects further divided into eighteen sects.

shikantaza (只管打坐): Dōgen's expression for zazen as just sitting, or "nothing but sitting."

Shōbōgenzō (正法眼蔵): *Shōbōgenzō* is the major work of Dōgen. The title literally means the true dharma eye treasury.

Shōbōgenzō Zuimonki (*Sayings of Dōgen*): A collection of Dōgen's informal talks recorded by his dharma successor Ejo between 1235 and 1237.

shuku (粥): *Shuku* is rice gruel. It also refers to breakfast in the Zen monastery.

Song China (J. Sō, 宋): The Song is the name of the dynasty that governed China from 960 to 1279.

Steward: See administrator.

Store officers (J. *kusu*, 庫司): The store officers are the six stewards (*roku-chiji*), whose quarters and duties are in the storehouse.

Suttanipata (経集): The *Suttanipata* is one of the oldest Buddhist scriptures, a part of the Pali canon. The *Suttanipata* is a collection of many short sutras.

tangaryō (旦過寮): The room where traveling monks stay when visiting or before they are accepted into the monks' hall in a monastery.

tenzo: See cook.

Tathagata (J. *nyorai*, 如来): One of the ten epithets of the Buddha. It literally means "thus come" or "thus gone."

three jewels (J. *sanbō*, 三宝): The Buddha, dharma, and sangha are called the three jewels or treasures in Buddhism. All Buddhists take refuge in these three jewels.

Tiantong Monastery (天童寺): The monastery in China where Dogen practiced with his teacher Rujing (J. Nyojō).

vihara (J. *shōja* 精舎): The Sanskrit word for a monastery or temple.

Vinaya (J. *ritsuzō*, 律蔵): The Vinaya contains the Buddhist monastic regulations along with stories about why these regulations were established by the Buddha. It is one part of the Tripitaka or "three baskets" of Buddhist teaching. The other two baskets are the sutra pitaka (the sutras or teachings of the Buddha) and the abidharma pitaka (the commentaries on the sutras).

way-seeking mind (J. *bodaishin*, 菩提心、or *dōshin*, 道心): Way-seeking mind is a translation of the Sanskrit word *bodhi-citta*, which means awakening or aspiration to seek awakening. People who arouse this mind are called bodhisattvas.

Chinese and Japanese Names

Chinese

Baizhang Huaihai, 720–814 (百丈懷海, Hyakujō Ekai). A Dharma successor of Mazu, he compiled the first regulations for a Zen monastery and insisted, "A day of no work is a day of no eating." Teacher of Huangbo and Guishan.

Baoning Renyong, 11th century (保寧仁勇, Honei Jinyu). A Dharma successor of Yangqi Fanghui, who was the founder of one of the two main branches of Rinzai Zen.

Dajian Huineng, 638–713 (大鑑惠能, Daikan Enō). The famous Sixth Ancestor of Chan (five generations after the founder Bodhidharma), whose biography and teachings were expounded in the Platform Sutra. All the main lines of Zen derive from his dharma heirs.

Daowu Yuanzhi, 769–835 (道吾圓智, Dōgo Enchi). Daowu was a student of Baizhang, and then became dharma heir of Yaoshan Weiyan, along with Daowu's biological and dharma brother Yunyan, was the teacher of Dongshan, founder of the Caodong/Sōtō lineage.

Deshan Xuanjian, 780–865 (德山宣鑑, Tokusan Senkan). Teacher of Xuefeng, he is famous for his animated style of teaching by shouting and striking his students. Previously a lecturer of the Diamond Sutra, he burnt his books after being awakened to Chan by an old woman selling tea cakes.

Dongshan Liangjie, 807–69 (洞山良价, Tōzan Ryōkai). Founder of the Caodong (Sōtō) lineage, the branch of Chan later transmitted by Dōgen to Japan. He is author of the "Song of the Jewel-Mirror Samadhi" (Hōkyōzanmai).

Dongshan Shiuchu, 910–90 (洞山守初, Tōzan Shusho). A disciple of Yunmen.

Fushan Fayuan, 991–1067 (浮山法遠, Fusan Hōon). Dharma heir of Shexian Guisheng, despite having been previously expelled from his assembly. He also saved the Caodong/Sōtō lineage from extinction when Dayang Qingxuan was going to die without a dharma heir. Fushan was in the responsibility of publicly proclaiming the Sōtō style in addition to his Rinzai lineage from Guisheng. However, he was able later to transmit the Sōtō lineage from Dayang to his own student, Touzi Yiqing.

Guishan Lingyou, 771–853 (為山靈祐, Isan Reiyu). A disciple of Baizhang Huaihai, Guishan was the founder, along with his disciple Yangshan Huiji, of one of the five lineages of classical Chinese Zen Buddhism, the Guiyang line (Igyō in Japanese).

Jianyuan Zhongxing, n.d. (漸源仲興, Zengen Chūkō). Dharma heir of Daowu Yuanzhi.

Jiashan Shanhui, 805–81 (夾山善会, Kassan Zenne). Dharma heir of Chuanzi Dechung, who was nicknamed "the boatman" because he lived in the world as a ferryman after the persecution of Buddhism in 842. After transmitting the dharma to Jiashan, he overturned the boat and disappeared into the water.

Nanyue Huairang, 677–744 (南嶽懷攘, Nangaku Ejō). One of the most important disciples of the Six Ancestor Dajian Huineng.

Qingyuan Xingsi, d. 740 (青原行思, Seigen Gyōshi). One of the two main disciples of the Sixth Ancestor, along with Nanyue Huairang.

Shishuang Qingzhu, 807–88 (石霜慶諸, Sekisō Keisho). Dharma heir of Daowu Yuanzhi, who had been tenzo for Guishan. Shishuang Qingzhu's assembly was noted for always sleeping sitting up, and so was called the "Dead Tree Hall."

Shitou Xiqian, 700–790 (石頭希遷, Sekitō Kisen). Shitou was two generations after the Sixth Ancestor. He wrote the long poem "Sandōkai" (Unifying of Sameness and Differences), which is still important in the Sōtō tradition.

Taiyuan Fu, 9th cent. (太原孚, Taigen Fu). A disciple of Xuefeng who was awakened by a tenzo from Jiashan.

Tiantong Rujing, 1163–1228 (天童如淨, Tendō Nyojō). Dōgen's teacher. Dōgen practiced with him for three years at Mt. Tiantong in China and received the Caodong/Sōtō transmission from him.

Wuzhuo Wenxi, 821–900 (無着文喜, Mujaku Bunki). Dharma heir of Yangshan, he was known for his conversations with Manjushri, the bodhisattva of wisdom.

Xuedou Zhongxian, 980–1052 (雪竇重顯, Secchō Jūken). A master in the Yunmen lineage and noted poet, his selection of one hundred cases with verse commentaties was the basis for the famous *Blue Cliff Record* (*Hekigan Roku*).

Xuefeng Yicun, 822–908 (雪峰義存, Seppō Gison). After serving as tenzo at many temples, he finally became the heir of Deshan Xuanjian. Xuefeng was the teacher of Yunmen and was the third-generation ancestor of Fayan, founders of two of the five classical Chan lineages.

Yunmen Wenyan, 864–949 (雲門文偃, Unmon Bunen). Dharma successor of Xuefeng and founder of one of the five houses of Chan, he is famous for his pithy responses to questions and is featured in many of the classical koans.

Yunyan Tansheng, 781–841 (雲巖曇晟, Ungan Donjō). Dharma heir of Yaoshan, after serving twenty years as Baizhang's jisha without having realization (unlike his older biological brother Daowu, who was also a student of Baizhang and Yaoshan). Yunyan later was the teacher of Dongshan Liangjie, who honored Yunyan as his master over other, more famous teachers he had studied with, because Yunyan "never explained anything to him directly."

Zhaozhou Congshen, 778–897 (趙州諗従, Jōshū Jūshin). Dharma heir of Nanquan Puyuan, he is considered one of the all-time great Zen masters and is the source of many of the classic koans, such as his response to the question, "Does a dog have buddha nature?"

Japanese

Butsuju Myōzen, 1184–1225 (仏樹明全). Disciple of Yōjō Eisai, who introduced Rinzai Zen to Japan. Myōzen was Dōgen's original Zen teacher in Japan and they went to China together. Unfortunately Myozen died in China.

Daichi Sokei, 1290–1366 (大智祖継). Daichi was ordained by Kangan Giin, a disciple of Dōgen. He went to China and practiced there for eleven years. Daichi is famous for his poetry.

Eihei Dōgen, 1200–1253 (永平道元). Dōgen was ordained as a Tendai monk when he was thirteen years old. He practiced Zen under Myōzen at Kenninji, which was founded by Eisai. Dōgen went to China with Myōzen in 1223 and stayed there for five years. After receiving dharma transmission from Rujing, Dōgen went back to Japan in 1227. He founded Kōshōji in 1233 and stayed there for ten years. Dōgen moved to Echizen and established Eiheiji in 1243 and lived there the rest of his life. He died in 1253.

Eisai. See Yōjō Eisai.

Ejō. See Koun Ejō.

Koun Ejō, 1198–1280 (孤雲懐奘). Dōgen's dharma heir and the second abbot of Eiheiji. The copies Ejō made of Dōgen's writings, including Shōbōgenzō, are in many cases the sole surviving copy of his writings.

Myōzen. See Butsuju Myōzen.

Kōdō Sawaki, 1880–1965 (沢木興道). Kōshō Uchiyama's teacher.

Tettsu Gikai, 1219–1309 (徹通義介). Dharma heir of Koun Ejō and the third abbot of Eiheiji. Gikai founded Daijōji in Kanazawa, Ishikawa prefecture. Keizan Jōkin was Gikai's disciple.

Yōjō Eisai, 1141–1215 (葉上栄西). Eisai went to China and introduced Rinzai Zen to Japan. Dōgen practiced at Kenninji with Eisai's disciple Myōzen.

Acknowledgments

A great many people have contributed to bringing this book to you, freely giving their effort for love of the dharma, and the editors are grateful to all of them. The first layer of donors were the authors of the essays and all the people who helped them at their temples and schools, the publisher, and Eiheiji.

The second layer is the many people connected with the international commemorative events for the eight hundredth anniversary of Dōgen Zenji's birth and the seven hundred fiftieth anniversary of his death, who wanted to bring this book to the United States. This group includes people who have been part of the commemorative committee at Eiheiji, and all the other priests at Eiheiji who have encouraged, supported, and funded this project. We also would like to express our appreciation to the Sōtō Zen Administrative Office and Education Center of North America for their cooperation.

At the third layer the circle widens, and the editors would like to thank all who helped us with the actual work of this book; we apologize for anyone inadvertently unmentioned. The ground work was laid first by Rev. Shin'etsu Fukushima, who was a member of Eiheiji's international commemorative committee, and then by Rev. Shōhaku Okamura, who lives in the United States and heads the Sōtō Zen Education Center in San Francisco. The initial translation drafts of the essays were done by Japanese priests working in the United States: Gengo Akiba, Griffith Foulk, Isshō Fujita, Eishin Ikeda, Wakō Katō, Kōshi Kuwahara, Shōhaku Okumura, and Taiken Yokoyama. They were helped by many others, including Rev. Shuichi Tom Kurai of Sōzenji in Montebello, California, Naoko Horii, Carla Price, Geff Shūdō Brown, Geffery Tesshin Brooks, and Rev. Chikō Clelia Corona. Their drafts were sent for editing to us, the four editors, Taigen Dan Leighton, John McRae, Shōhaku Okumura, and Jisho Warner. Shuichi Kurai and Taiken Yokoyama greatly helped our work of producing an integrated working draft at a three-week translation workshop in 1999 in

Bloomington, Indiana (where McRae teaches in the Religious Studies department at Indiana University). When Jisho Warner reedited the volume she was much assisted by Kōshin Steve Kelly and Kenshō Miyamae of the Sōtō Zen Education Center. Taiken Yokoyama organized this project as the contact person for Eiheiji, the translators, and the editors. Rev. Ikki Nambara of Sōkōji in San Francisco helped us with computer work on the manuscript. We are grateful also to Jeffrey R. Hunter of Weatherhill for accepting the book for publication and for his helpful comments.

Contributors

Names of Japanese people are given here in the traditional Japanese order, beginning with the family name.

Authors

Aoyama Shundō (青山俊董, b. 1933). Reverend Aoyama was born in Ichinomiya in Aichi prefecture. She was ordained when she was fifteen years old and practiced at Aichi Senmon Nisōdō. Then she studied at Komazawa University and finished graduate school and Kyōkakenshūsho (Sōtō-shū Educational Research Institute). She has been abbess of Aichi Senmon Nisōdō since 1976. In 1984 and 1997 she visited Zen centers in the U.S. She is also the resident priest of Muryōji in Nagano prefecture. One of her books is available in English, *Zen Seeds: Reflection of a Female Priest* (Kōsei), and another is in preparation.

Hashimoto Zengan (橋本禅巌, 1898–1994). Reverend Hashimoto was a disciple of Rev. Arai Sekizen, who was the abbot of Sōjiji, which is one of the two head temples and training centers of the Sōtō school along with Eiheiji. Hashimoto founded his own temple Kenshōji in Niigata in 1935, mainly by doing mendicant practice.

Hata Egyoku (秦慧玉, 1896–1985). Reverend Hata was born in Kōbe. After his father died, he was ordained by Rev. Hata Eshō when he was eight years old and later received dharma transmission from the same teacher. He graduated from Sōtōshū Daigakurin (present-day Komazawa University) in 1920. He also practiced at a Rinzai monastery, Shōgenji, in Ibuka, Gifu prefecture. He taught at Urawa Kōtōgakkō for twenty years, beginning in 1926, and at Komazawa University for thirty-three years beginning in 1927. In 1958, he became godō (senior teacher) at Eiheiji and served for three years. In 1965, he became abbot of Chūōji in Sapporo, Hokkaidō. He was the abbot of Eiheiji from 1976 to 1985. In 1979, he visited Hawaii and the West coast of the United

States for the 700th anniversary of the death of the second abbot of Eiheiji, Koun Ejō.

Katagiri Dainin (片桐大忍, 1928–90). Reverend Katagiri was born in Osaka. After ordination he trained at Eiheiji for three years under Rev. Hashimoto Ekō, and then attended Komazawa University, where he received a master's degree. He came to the U.S. in 1963, to Zenshūji temple in Los Angeles, and later moving to San Francisco, where he assisted Rev. Suzuki Shunryū first at Sōkōji temple and then at the San Francisco Zen Center. In 1972 he moved to Minnesota and founded the Minnesota Zen Meditation Center. He developed the center to include both a city center in Minneapolis and a seasonal monastery and training center, Hōkyōji, in the country. Two books of his teachings have been published, *Returning to Silence* and *You Have to Say Soemthing* (both by Shambhala).

Kurebayashi Kōdō (樽林晧堂, 1893–1988). Professor Kurebayashi was born in Shizuoka prefecture and was ordained by Rev. Toyama Soei in Tokyo. Toyama was a student of the famous master, Nishiari Bokusan and he transcribed Nishiari's formal talks on the *Shōbōgenzō*. Kurebayashi later edited the transcription and published it as *Shōbōgenzō Keiteki* (Guide to *Shōbōgenzō*). This book is still one of the most authoritative commentaries on Dōgen's *Shōbōgenzō*. Kurebayashi graduated from Sōtōshū Daigakurin (now Komazawa University) in 1917. He practiced at Eiheiji with Rev. Oka Sōtan, and at Eigenji and Shichikurin Gakudō Antaiji in Kyoto with Rev. Kishizawa Ian. From 1927, he taught at Komazawa University. He served as president of Komazawa University from 1968 to 1975.

Mizuno Kōgen (水野弘元, b.1901). Professor Mizuno was born in Saga prefecture. In 1925 he graduated from Tokyo University with a major in Indian philosophy. Mizuno taught at Tokyo University and Keio University. In 1962 Mizuno became a professor at Komazawa University. He became the president of Komazawa University in 1982, and now he is a professor emeritus. He was one of the best-known scholars of Early Buddhism in Japan and made a Pali dictionary. A few of his books have been translated into English, including, *Buddhist Sutras* and *The Beginnings of Buddhism* (both from Kōsei).

Niwa Renpō (丹羽廉芳, 1905–93). Reverend Niwa was born in Shizuoka prefecture and was ordained in 1916 when he was twelve years old. He graduated from Tokyo University with a major in Indian philosophy. He practiced at Shichikurin Antaiji in 1931 and studied Tendai teachings at Otani University in Kyoto. In 1933, he finished priest training at Eiheiji. He served as vice abbot of Eiheiji for nine years beginning in 1976 and then was the abbot of Eiheiji from 1985 to 1993.

Shinno Kōryō (新野光亮, 1937–86). Reverend Shinno was resident priest of Tokujōji in Chiba prefecture. Shinno finished the doctoral course at Komazawa University, practiced at Eiheiji and finished Shūgaku Kenkyūsho (The Institute for Sōtō Zen Studies). He studied with Prof. Kurebayashi. Shinno was killed in a traffic accident in 1986 when he was 49 years old.

Shinohara Hisao (篠原寿雄, b. 1924). Professor Shinohara graduated from Komazawa University in 1946. He served as an assistant at Kyoto University and became a professor of Komazawa University. Presently he is a professor emeritus of Komazawa University. His field was Chinese philosophy and Zen Buddhism, and he has published an annotated version of the *Eihei Shingi*.

Uchiyama Kōshō (内山興正, 1912–98). Reverend Uchiyama was born in Tokyo. He studied Western philosophy at Waseda University and was ordained by Rev. Sawaki Kōdō in 1941. He was the abbot of Antaiji from 1965 to 1975, where he taught many Westerners as well as Japanese. After retired from Antaiji, Uchiyama lived at Nōkein in Uji, Kyoto. His books translated into English are *From the Zen Kitchen to Enlightenment* (Weatherhill), *The Zen Teaching of 'Homeless' Kōdō* (Sōtōshū Shūmuchō), *Opening the Hand of Thought* (Penguin), and *The Wholehearted Way* (Tuttle). Further translations are in process.

Translators

Akiba Gengo (秋葉玄吾). General Director of Sōtō Zen Administrative Office of North America, and abbot of Zenshūji in Los Angeles and Kōjin-an, Oakland, California.

Griffith Foulk. Professor, Sarah Lawrence College.

Fujita Isshō (藤田一照). Resident priest of Pioneer Valley Zendo in Massachusetts.

Ikeda Eishin (池田永晋). Resident priest of Beantown Sangha in Massachusetts.

Katō Wakō (加藤和光). Retired Professor, Nagoya University of Foreign Studies, and supporting priest of Zenshūji, Los Angeles.

Kuwahara Kōshi (桑原弘之). Counselor of Sōtō Zen Administrative Office of North America, and priest of Zenshūji, Los Angeles.

Okumura Shōhaku (奥村正博). Director of Sōtō Zen Education Center, San Francisco, and head priest and teacher of Sanshin Zen Community.

Yokoyama Taiken (横山泰賢). Secretary of Sōtō Zen Education Center and priest and teacher of Sanshin Zen Community.

Editors

Taigen Dan Leighton. Priest of San Francisco Zen Center, in California.
John McRae. Professor of Buddhist Studies, Indiana University.
Okumura Shōhaku. Director of Sōtō Zen Education Center.
Jisho Warner. Resident priest and teacher of Stone Creek Zendo, in Sebastopol, California.

The "weathermark" identifies this book as a production of Weatherhill, Inc., publishers of fine books on Asia and the Pacific. Editorial supervision: Jeffrey Hunter. Book and cover design: Noble & Israel Design. Production Supervision: Bill Rose. Printing and Binding: R.R. Donnelly. The typeface used is Caecilia.